In Loving Hands

In Loving Hands

*How the Rights for Young Children Living in
Children's Homes Offer Hope and Happiness in
Today's World*

In Collaboration with World Forum Foundation

Elsa Chahin with Anna Tardos

**and
Other Contributors**

Library of Congress Control Number:		2017905445
ISBN:	Hardcover	978-1-5434-1433-2
	Softcover	978-1-5434-1432-5
	eBook	978-1-5434-1431-8

Cover photo by Etienne Moine, Casa Ami, Ecuador

Print information available on the last page.

Rev. date: 09/12/2017

To order additional copies of this book, contact:
Xlibris
1-888-795-4274
www.Xlibris.com
Orders@Xlibris.com
758365

*For Leo, Éva, Ágnes, and Gábor—their love sustains us—
and for the children of the world, they are our hope . . .*

CONTENTS

PART THREE

Dedication

With special recognition to the life and work of Dr. Emmi Pikler, this book is also dedicated to the loving memories of Dr. Myriam David, Dr. Judit Falk, Éva Kálló, Dr. Mária Vincze, Laura Briley, and the many others who have devoted their lives to making a difference in the upbringing of our most vulnerable children. Their work and invaluable contributions leave a legacy of hope, with their unflagging and compassionate commitment the driving force behind this book.

Acknowledgments

We would like to thank and acknowledge all of our associates who collaborated in the writing of this book by donating their time and expertise. Their efforts in making a difference in the lives of children reared in residential care are helping to plant a seed for world peace.

Special mention also goes to award-winning journalist, Victoria Looseleaf for her editorial contributions to this book.

In addition, we would like to express our appreciation to the World Forum Foundation, and co-founders Bonnie and Roger Neugebauer, for their invitation to write this book. The mission of the World Forum Foundation is to promote an ongoing global exchange of ideas on the delivery of quality services for young children in diverse settings.

Authors' Note

For the purpose of clarity and ease of reading, authors will use the singular and/or plural personal pronouns interchangeably when expressing our voices; and when we refer to a child, it will be in the masculine; the caregiver[1] will always be referred to in the feminine.

This book also contains articles by experts from around the world, who are interested in improving conditions of children living in institutions. In the first two parts, the book is supplemented mostly by excerpts from articles by Dr. Emmi Pikler and her team of experts (*Falk, Hevesi, Kálló, Tardos, Vincze*) that were originally included in the book *Bringing Up and Providing Care for Infants and Toddlers in an Institution (BUPCITI)* published by the Pikler-Lóczy Association for Young Children, Budapest, Hungary.

---

1   Caregiver refers to a trained person who provides care to children under the age of three and contributes to the physical and emotional well-being of children during their stay at a children's home.

I speak not for myself but for those without a voice . . . those who have fought for their rights . . . their right to live in peace, their right to be treated with dignity, their right to equality of opportunity, their right to be educated. When the whole world is silent, even one voice becomes powerful.

—**Malala Yousafzai,** youngest-ever Nobel Prize laureate

Foreword

Peter Mangione PhD[2]

Early brain development is often thought of as a matter of building connections in the brain. But the developing brain also makes connections with the surrounding interpersonal world. The quality of connections with others influences the quality of connections within the brain. Daniel Siegel expresses the simple yet eloquent link between early relationship quality and the developing brain when he states, "Human connections create brain connections."

At birth, the human brain is not fully formed. In fact, the human baby comes into the world in a state of prolonged helplessness, which allows the brain to develop. To survive, the baby needs to be nurtured. Quite naturally, the baby seeks human connection, to be protected, to be fed, and to learn. In a caring relationship, the developing child can feel secure and, when respected as a competent person, can explore and make discoveries about self, others, and the physical environment. The baby also learns from others.

Relationships offer to children the predictable routines of daily life, rules for living, the complexity and wonder of communication, and the warmth of care and love. Through being connected to others, the young child not only grows to be autonomous, but also part of the human community. And the baby's brain has the kind of stimulation that enables it to grow and build the capacity to continue learning and cooperate with others.

---

2   See CONTRIBUTORS page for Dr. Mangione's biography.

Many children enter the world and experience early childhood in a loving family. The emotional security that children develop through caring familial relationships and the possibilities for learning about life through making connections with others is a birthright for them. Of course, not all children necessarily experience the birthright of a loving family. For one reason or another, they may find themselves in an institution, without a family to nurture them, and many without meaningful connections with other humans and the possibility of learning through those connections. But like all children, they are born with developing brains that will thrive in nurturing, enduring relationships. And like all children, they have the right to the relational experiences that provide a foundation for self-determination and constructive participation in human communities.

This important book expresses children's fundamental right to conditions that support their development in the following way:

All children living in institutions have the right to be highly valued as group members and also as individuals so they can experience a complete (developmentally and emotionally sound) childhood throughout their stay.

Indeed, a developmentally and emotionally sound childhood is the right of every child. For many, what we consider the essentials of childhood is taken for granted. So much so we do not articulate those essentials as rights. But for children in institutions, cut off from the way human society most often nurtures its youngest, we need to spell out the essentials—the rights of every child.

These essentials include physical well-being and health: "nutritious food, appropriate clothing, personal belongings, clean environments, and fresh air." In my view, even more important is the second right stated by this volume's authors: "All children have the right to develop an individual, personal, loving, and supportive relationship with the adults who take care of them."

An essential part of developmentally and emotionally harmonious relationships for children is to be cared for by adults who are responsive to their individual needs and give them time to appreciate and learn from personalized nurturance. Such relationships, as the fourth right sets forth, protect children from aggression—"open or hidden, verbal or physical"—and affirm the right of all humans to be accepted and respected. The right to continuity and stability of personal relationships forms the bedrock for sturdy development, providing children predictable experience, which enables their developing brains to anticipate what will happen and learn how to act skillfully and appropriately.

The right to be oneself and act on one's natural inclination to move and play freely, discover surroundings, and develop capacities complements the right of sound, stable relationships. Nurturing adults are sensitive to this right for self-determined activity and offer children safe, engaging environments to initiate movement and exploration, and engage in play and discovery. Through self-determined action, children discover possibilities within themselves, and practice and master emerging skills. In doing so, they have an opportunity to realize the fundamental right of seeing themselves as capable individuals who are regarded positively by others.

The right to be accepted and respected as an individual works hand in hand with support and respect for individuality. All children differ from one another. Each follows a distinct developmental path at an individual pace. In articulating the eighth right, the authors make a strong case for the right of children to have their individual developmental pace supported and respected. Without the right to develop in their own way, at their own pace, children's natural inclination to move and make discoveries and their confidence in themselves can be easily undermined.

An integral part of creating a sense of self is the development of an autobiographical self. As children grow, they define themselves in relation to others. Who they are and where they come from are fundamentally important to them. As the authors state: "All children have the right to know their personal history." For children who are separated from their families to experience this right, they need to be supported in order to have continued contact with their families.

This volume makes clear that the connection with others is the thread that binds together all ten rights of children.

Though autonomous, children ultimately need an enduring connection with others—the security and sense of wholeness that come from living in a loving family. The larger human community is responsible for ensuring this right to a loving family. In affirming this right of each child in a way that is fully in harmony with the developing individual, we are affirming the rights of all children and honoring everyone's life. Just as important, we are supporting the capacity of today's children to develop into adults who will respect and support the rights of the next generation of children.

In the pages that follow, the authors clearly describe these rights, set forth a compelling rationale for them, and illuminate how to respect and uphold them for all children.

We are born of love; love is our mother.

—Rumi

We Must Help

Some Thoughts about Children's Homes

By Jason Bell[3]

None of us chooses the event or the circumstances of our birth. To arrive on this planet, to survive the trauma of birth and begin the long journey to independence and adulthood—all are, in the most profound sense, the gifts of a sequence of miracles.

Birth is, one might say, a common miracle. There are now nearly 7.5 billion human beings on the globe, and during the last century alone, our numbers have grown from 1.65 billion to 6 billion.[4]

If those numbers make our individuality seem less special, we should remember our real origins: Every newborn, every child, is forged in the stars. All our bodies come together from exactly the same elements that compose the universe, in nearly the same proportions: oxygen, hydrogen, carbon, and nitrogen.[5] And those elements combine to make each of us into the collective genus, *Homo sapiens*.

We are all one species: No race or nationality is inherently different from or better than the rest. These things all humans have in common. But that's where human equality ends.

Consider all the things that happen in order to create a healthy, compassionate, and functioning adult human being. Think, for

---

3   Jason Bell is an award-winning a poet and writer. See CONTRIBUTORS page for his biography.

4   http://www.worldometers.info/world-population/

5   http://www.buffalo.edu/ubreporter/archive/2010_03_31/tyson_dss

instance, of the long train of good decisions, hard work, and sheer happenstance that enables you to even read these words. From the instant of our conception, we, who can read, love, think, and walk, have also run a gauntlet of chance and choice to become who we are.

If a child isn't born into a loving and durable family, who will provide these necessary years of care? Estimates vary widely, but by all counts from nongovernmental organizations (NGOs) plus charities and state institutions, there are more than 130 million infants and children in the world for whom the answer to that question is uncertain.

Orphaned at birth or in infancy, abandoned for economic reasons or from wars and epidemics, these humans face staggering obstacles and perils—all through no fault or action of their own.

By current estimates, there are between 130 and 153 million orphans in the world,[6] with 5,760 more children orphaned each day.[7] Every year the "system" of worldwide institutions caring for orphans "ages out," with 14.5 million more children who are only sixteen years old, and 230 million children under age five worldwide (about one in three), whose births have never been officially recorded.[8]

These facts warrant our attention, compassion, and humility in the face of the enormous problems that orphaned infants and children face, although being born or growing up an orphan does not necessarily lead to a life of failure and unhappiness.

Indeed, a short list of those who have overcome this early deprivation includes

---

6   http://www.unicef.org/statistics/

7   http://ccainstitute.org/resources/fact-sheets

8   http://www.data.unicef.org/corecode/uploads/document6/uploaded_pdfs/
     corecode/Birth_Registration_lores_final_24.pdf

- Simón Bolívar, Latin American independence leader, orphaned, age 8
- Alexander Hamilton, U.S. founding father, orphaned, age 13
- Herbert Hoover, 31st U.S. president, orphaned, age 9
- Andrew Jackson, U.S. president, orphaned, age 14
- Benito Juarez, Mexican president, orphaned, age 3
- Nelson Mandela, president of South Africa, raised as a ward
- Eleanor Roosevelt, U.S. First Lady, civil-rights activist, orphaned, age 10
- Ella Fitzgerald, one of the finest female jazz singer of all time, orphaned age 15
- Marilyn Monroe, American actress, orphaned age nine

But this small sampling of men and women who have achieved greatness or renown after orphanhood tells us little about how to replicate their successes. How were they saved? How were they educated? Were they raised in institutions or by a sibling or extended family? Did they spend time in a foster family? Were there villages, tribal customs, or cultural practices that nurtured or protected them?

Furthermore, how should we help? Certainly, the first stage can be personal education and empathy, and the next steps will be determined by skills and whatever resources each individual can bring to bear. One thing is certain though: Everyone lives or travels near children in need of assistance, and becoming aware of their presence is a great beginning.

Love somebody. Just one person. And then spread that to two. And as many as you can. You'll see the difference it makes.

—**Oprah Winfrey**

Prologue

Our Loving Hands

The way we use our hands, how we touch the infant, how we convey our message of love through touch, will have repercussions on how a baby will come to see the world and how his brain will eventually be wired.

This is a love that comes through a gentle, nurturing and affectionate respectful touch, and awareness; a love that can be grasped by the daily interactions between a young child and the one that cares for him, can sustain him by the mere sense of belonging. This kind of loving awareness can lead our young on a path to fulfillment, or at the very least, this love can keep them from trouble.

In short, we are talking about a love that allows a child in an institution, without a mother or a family, to not merely survive, but also to thrive.

Having been influenced by Dr. Emmi Pikler's research and life's work, we will support our writings by presenting Piklerian ideas, as well as including excerpts and citations by experts that worked closely with Dr. Pikler. Although there are other institutions around the world whose children grow up with positive experiences and have fond memories as adults, the Pikler Institute provided a detailed description of its methods, and thus, we found it beneficial to support our writing with their findings.

Pikler affirmed that babies should never be treated mechanically nor handled like an object. She believed that the hands constituted the infant's first connection to the world and, depending on how these hands administered care, would result in how the infant would come to view the world.

Pikler also talked about moving in ceremonious slowness, as our rhythm and slow pace send a message to the infant as well. Babies do not need fancy furniture or the latest toys. The simplest of all things required for their secure upbringing are the patient and loving hands of the adults that care for them. These loving hands lay the foundation of how they will come to build trust in the world and are a gift they will carry with them throughout adulthood.

Hands are also a symbol for respectful relationships. Through the gestures of offering, calling, and asking for something, they convey a message and an invitation for cooperation. Each of these gestures is a half-finished movement of expectation. Each expresses an expectation on the child's behalf, a possibility of choice. These half-finished movements offer children the opportunity to put forth an answer out of their own volition.

The act of asking for something with our hands plays a particularly important role in the togetherness with infants and toddlers. As with calling and offering, the movement that asks for something is the expression of a peaceful approach to the child. It indicates that the person who is asking will not resort to violence in order to assert her wish. It is an expression of the fact that the adult doesn't intend to act alone. Rather, she waits for the child to put something into the open hand, such as a slipper that he just took off or a tissue with which he just wiped his nose.

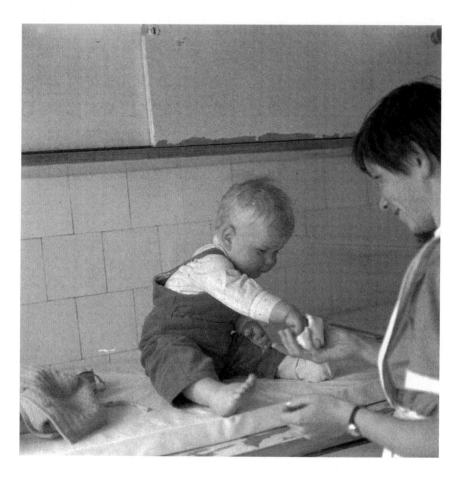

A gentle and patient hand elicits cooperation at the Pikler@ Institute.
Photo by Marian Reismann from the Pikler archives.

That asking, expecting attitude of the adult offers the infant the possibility of decision, the possibility to meet the adult's expectations out of his own free will. This is how the adult becomes the role model for the child. If the adult grabs or takes things from the child instead of asking, one would not expect a child to ask his playmate for a coveted toy instead of just grabbing it from him.

It is often easier to speak to a child with a gentle tone of voice than to hold him and care for him with mindful and aware hands.

It is because the adult's hands are so important to a child's rearing, and because hands convey a very important message to young children, that we chose the words "loving *hands*" in our title.

Indeed, hands can be a symbol of attentive, tactful, and loving care.

How This Book Came to Be: A Brief History of *In Loving Hands*

The Working Group for the Rights of Children in Children's Homes was launched at the 2009 World Forum in Belfast, Northern Ireland, and was headed by Laura Briley,[9] who passed away in 2013. The Working Group was attended by individuals from 10 countries who work in institutions and/or support and train professionals that work in institutions.

We continued to meet over the next few years, and in April, 2014, we convened at the World Forum on Early Care and Education in Puerto Rico. Our main focus was to finalize ideas for a book to guide professionals working in the area of children's homes around the world.

The Working Group of Pikler/Lóczy Association Hungary (Éva Kálló, Katalin Hevesi, and Anna Tardos) wrote the declaration of the 10 rights of young children living in children's homes for this book.

We invited colleagues and other professionals working with children's homes to participate in this book. These contributors from

---

9   See Laura Briley's tribute after closing words from Anna

around the globe provided thoughtful commentary for the rights, as well as offering in-depth looks at their programs.

Their voices prove that, regardless of cultural differences and customs and despite unfortunate beginnings, these children are being offered a healthy start to life.

We wrote this book precisely because we have seen that there is hope for children living in institutions or children's homes, and although, unfortunately, this is not always the case, there are children who can use their struggles to build resilience and grow up with good moral character. Still, it is up to us to provide support to all the children in order that they flourish—mentally, emotionally, and physically.

And with many children around the world still living in institutions, we understand that it is troublesome to implement conditions that offer these children a healthy upbringing. Research has proven that institutions are unnatural and artificial environments and may, therefore, pose dangerous circumstances.

René Spitz (1887–1974) was a Viennese-born psychiatrist and psychoanalyst who conducted extensive research about hospitalism, a pediatric diagnosis used to describe young children who failed to thrive in hospital settings and also in children's homes when living there for long periods without their mothers. (The mortality rate in children's homes was also markedly higher.)

It was proven (Spitz, 1945) that children suffered symptoms such as slow gross motor development and delay in language acquisition, as well as insufficient weight gain because of lack of social interaction with the people caring for them. Interestingly enough, it was also found that children residing in hospitals with little financial resources (unable to afford incubators, for example) were not as affected, since medical staff was forced to hold infants in their arms.

Based on this research, it was found that it was impossible to grow up well without a mother. There was a general opinion, which still prevails, that all infants' homes are harmful and that children should be placed in foster care. This has led to the closure of many infants' homes, with this idea having grown into a global movement.

Unfortunately, the foster care system doesn't solve all of the problems. Procedures can delay a baby or child finding a proper placement. By the time the system can do something, children will have had to wait in order to receive the proper care they deserve (not all countries offer foster care). The situation is complex; the foster care system doesn't guarantee that the child will be placed in the proper home, or not be passed from family to family, or that the child himself will be able to fit into the family.

And as long as we have some children living in institutions, we have to work to improve the care being provided in institutional settings.

For this reason, we must observe how children in institutions are being treated. By changing the usual ways institutions are caring for children in their everyday lives, infants' homes would not be harmful. Guidance then must be offered as to how this can be changed. Therefore, it is not only a deprivation of social interaction, but also an actively harmful way of interacting with young children that causes hospitalism.

Many children who suffer the consequences of war, disease, and natural disasters, or live in extreme poverty, are either unable to remain with their families or they don't have a family and are brought to live instead in an infants' home. As much as we wish for all children to live in loving families, the reality is that the world is rife with infants' homes, although they may not call themselves infants' homes.

Children are still orphaned, abandoned, or in need of temporary placement. And occasionally, there is an immediate need to offer a loving home before they are placed in foster homes, be put up for adoption, or returned to their birth families.

When Dr. Pikler founded a residential nursery in 1946 in Budapest, Hungary, she broke from the typical way of being with children in institutions, thus enabling her to achieve considerably different and positive results.

Because of this reality, we are advocating on behalf of children living in residential settings and are offering perspectives that will allow them to live in a safe and nurturing environment, while, at the same time, they can also receive responsive care from well-trained, educated, and nurturing adults.

And while we know that residential group care for children around the world needs to improve, there are exceptions that have proven successful.

Throughout the years, the Pikler Institute has had positive outcomes by creating a conscious system of caring for young children with the utmost respect. And like this institution, there are also several others around the world that are implementing similar practices that have positive outcomes. Their stories will be woven throughout this book.

As children living in residential settings deserve to have their voices heard, while, at the same time, having their rights respected, this book offers information and applicable tools that can be implemented toward improving the quality of care.

It is our intention to demonstrate that with the proper guidance, emotional support, and responsive presence of adults, children can then be given opportunities to thrive and grow up to be healthy and productive members of society—indistinguishable from a cross section of the general population.

Our mission is to support institutions in successfully caring for young children in group settings by providing them with information about best practices for children's homes and group care. This information is based on experience and research related to long-term beneficial outcomes.

PART ONE

Love and compassion are necessities, not luxuries. Without them, humanity cannot survive.

—Dalai Lama

Chapter 1.1

Words from Elsa Chahin

My dedication to this project stems from my personal experience, both as a mother and as a professional in the field of early childhood education, working directly with children and the adults that care for them. In addition, I am the current president of the nonprofit organization Pikler/Lóczy USA and World Forum Foundation's Working Group Leader of the Rights for Young Children Living in Children's Homes.

It is because of having personally witnessed the transformation of professionals working in residential care that I accepted the privilege of co-authoring this book with Anna Tardos, Dr. Emmi Pikler's daughter. Through stories and research, our goal is to help others achieve measurable results in their own settings.

I was fortunate to learn about Dr. Pikler's approach to caring for young children when I was pregnant with my son, Leonardo, in 1998. After reading Magda Gerber's books, we attended parent/infant guidance classes in RIE® (Resources for Infant Educarers), and having successfully applied these principles of respectful parenting with him, I then wanted to learn more.

I began to think of how many children might not have had a devoted mother to care for them and felt a responsibility to share what I had learned with others. I first wanted to implement Dr. Pikler's ideas with orphanages in my native Mexico.

In 2004, Tardos, former director of the Pikler Institute,[10] as well as my mentor and friend, encouraged me to start small and never give up. The first residential nursery I visited was an orphanage in Puebla, Mexico, that housed 50 infants, ages zero to three. The babies came from similar backgrounds as those living at the Pikler Institute:

---

10 We will be speaking about the Pikler Institute, also referred to as Lóczy, in the following chapters, including a brief history of this residential nursery established in 1946 and in operation until 2011.

abandoned, abused, or removed by an authority from their families because of extremely poor care or poverty.

My original idea was to "train" the staff according to the Pikler approach, but my first attempt to create a training curriculum was futile, as I had never observed their resident babies nor how they were being cared for. I needed to consider their culture, and although Mexican myself, I couldn't simply imply that they would easily relate to the Hungarian way of being.

To find an answer, I first needed to invest time in observing the babies and their caregiving interactions. By creating a dialogue with the caregivers and learning from them how they carried out their daily activities and cooperated with the infants, I was then better equipped to provide educated suggestions.

At the Pikler Institute, one caregiver took care of eight babies, whereas in Puebla, The ratio was 17 to one. In the morning, the youngest babies were taken out of their cribs and strapped into their infant seats. Lined up against the wall, all 17 of them waited their turns to be fed.

As the caregiver worked her way down the line, holding the bottle to the infant's mouth, it was surprising to see that the babies were not held during this crucial time. It wasn't that the caregivers didn't want to provide the best care; they simply didn't know how to manage.

After my observations and meeting with the institution's board of directors, I decided to create a "training-session" curriculum for the caregivers on the morning shift. We focused on the importance of one-on-one quality time, where talking to the infant during caregiving activities was also discussed, as well as the idea that the caregiver consider the infant a person.

I also wanted to impart the idea that slowing down is an imperative factor in quality care. When I returned the following day to work with the afternoon and weekend shifts, I first stopped to observe the infant room. It was mealtime, and babies awaited their daily feeding. It had been customary for the caregiver to simultaneously feed several babies at a time while propping the bottles into their mouths.

Something different happened as I was observing. The babies were taken out of their cribs and, one at a time, were being held during their feeding. Mariana, one of the caregivers that had been in my workshop the day before, was holding a baby in her arms, resting him gently on her lap.

As she momentarily glanced at me so as not to distract attention from the important task at hand, her eyes said to me that she understood how important it was for this baby, this individual, to be told through her touch, *"You are important to me."*

That was only the beginning. I then visited several more orphanages, where my dialogue with the caregivers resulted in positive experiences: Babies confined to cribs were given an opportunity to move freely in a safe space; they were given simple objects to interact with. In essence, they were given an invitation to be the creators of their explorations and movements.

It was during these caregiving routines that both adults and babies were able to feel that they were active participants. This was promoting the young children's resilience by fostering, through loving interactions, a positive image of themselves.

The caregivers in my seminars concluded that it is indeed possible to create a loving environment for children living in children's homes. In addition, through nurturing relationships, these children can thrive and build trust in themselves, the adults, and the world at large.

Also, by slowing down, caregivers became more present and aware during each moment of togetherness. With little or no financial resources, residential nurseries I have worked with have been able to make small positive changes in improving quality of care for their children.

Caregivers have been able to understand that it begins with their own self-awareness and internalization of how to better care for children with respect. Because this awareness is free, I feel that it can be applied to the poorest of circumstances and is determined by the adult willing to be mindfully attentive and have a special connection with each child.

There is also no need for fancy gadgets, gimmicks, or equipment, and despite the cultural differences among nationalities, it is clear that we all share one thing: our love for children and our commitment to improving their quality of life.

Children's lives can be touched in a beautiful way, thanks to the devoted and dedicated professionals that work with consciousness and awareness. It is our intention to share our mission on how to better care for babies with respect, furthering our dream that all young people can grow up feeling safe, secure, and with a sense of belonging.

Chapter 1.2

Love is the fruit in season at all times, and within the reach of every hand.

—Mother Teresa

Dr. Emmi Pikler: How She Revolutionized Infant and Toddler Care

Parts one and two of this book are primarily influenced by Dr. Emmi Pikler and her life's work because, simply put, her method, through decades of research in raising young children in institutions, has proven successful. Our intention is to share her ideas. We think that to know them can not only be informative, but also inspiring.

As there is no greater miracle than life itself, how do we express to each baby or young child under our care that we are grateful for their presence in our lives?

One of the simplest ways is to slow down during all care-related activities. This means that during every diaper change, every feeding, every time we dress him, bathe him, or put him to sleep, we are moving at a slower pace and synchronizing ourselves to *his* rhythm. By adapting to this rhythm, we are taking in what we are observing in each particular child.

Dr. Pikler's proposition on how to be respectful with the young stems from the simple idea of considering each child a unique individual from the first moment of life. Her observations led her to believe that a newborn could quickly turn into an object in the hands of an adult, if the adult caring for him was not attentive to his inner needs.

A baby needs time to adjust his body to what we are asking of him. As he anticipates what is about to happen, he can relax his tonus (the constant low-level activity of a body tissue, especially muscle tone) and actually become a participant during his care instead of a passive recipient.

We never want him to feel like he is an object. We may say things like, *"I am going to dress you now,"* and wait a little bit before performing the task.

As we proceed to put on his sweater, we may say, *"I am going to put this sleeve on your arm,"* and depending on this young child's developmental stage, we may even wait for him to give us his arm. We continue by asking for his other arm and by waiting for his physical response.

This process requires patience and should never be hurried. It is our job to offer babies and young children a peaceful beginning, one in which the adult slows down and follows each child's individual cues of readiness.

By following this process, we are showing responsiveness and presence: Through our articulated movements and gentle tone of voice, we are offering babies an invitation to participate and be the cocreators of their care. Slowing down may take a few more minutes than hurried care, but the outcome is a trusting baby, one who is willing to give us his disposition and attention, and thus discovers pleasure in the relationship.

As Dr. Pikler once wrote about the infant who participates actively in his care and lives in satisfactory emotional balance, he will also be active in his everyday life.

This is an investment of time with infinite positive results.

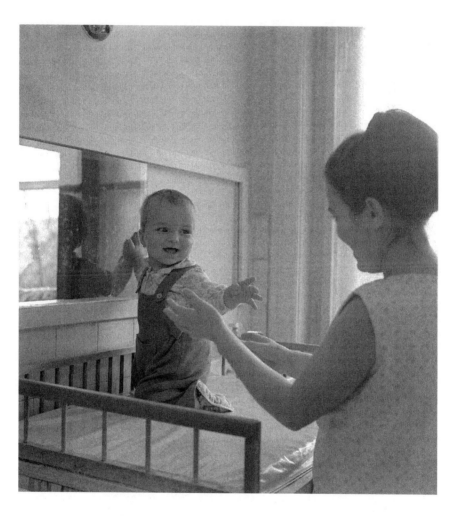

A shared moment during a caregiving interaction at the Pikler Institute. Photo by Marian Reismann from the Pikler archives.

Every interaction between an adult and an infant may be crucial for the development of a child's personality. It is up to us to decide what kind of world we want to create for children by modeling with our behavior. By choosing to be present, to be attentive, to be respectfully caring, we can show even the youngest children that we are responsive to them.

The following is an excerpt from an article written by Dr. Pikler. [11]

"Generally, the newborn infant is considered a helpless creature if he is unable to express his sense of well-being but who cries if he feels uncomfortable. If he is crying, he is to be appeased; if he is hungry, he needs to be fed. The infant is being nursed, caressed, and hugged, for he likes to be close to the human body. As for rearing, we have recently observed a growing intensity of "teaching" the infant. It is assumed that the more information that is fed to the baby, the better.

The infant is expected to persist in the positions into which he is regularly placed, to imitate simple operations demonstrated to him, to repeat what he has been repeatedly told.

Not only food, but also knowledge is being fed to the baby. As a rule, the adult decides what the baby has to know and when, also how he is to do things. He is trained to do so, induced to perform with more or less help from the adults. Less and less attention is paid to the infant's initiatives, to his signals. Hence, when these cues become scarcer, the child turns to imitation, to repetition, in practically all realms of life.

This type of education renders the child totally dependent on the adult, one who lacks self-reliance. This is generally considered a fundamental matter and not a consequence. This type of rearing is in contrast with the discoveries of recent investigations of the physical growth of infants."

11 Pikler, Emmi, *The competence of the infant*, Acta Paediatrica Academiae Scientiarum Hungaricae, Vol. 20 (2–3), 1970.

And though much progress has been made in the world since Dr. Pikler wrote those words, the fact remains that children living in institutions are still in danger of being harmed because of neglect. Different from a mother, a caregiver isn't providing care for her own child. She also cares for many children simultaneously. The care, therefore, can become very impersonal.

Spitz, James Robertson, and John Bowlby say that it is impossible to raise children well in institutions without maternal love (known as the maternal deprivation hypothesis) and that institutions cannot provide them with the right attention. They believed that a child could be damaged emotionally because of the lack of care.

Pikler's goal was to support children's well-being, keeping them emotionally and physically safe. She worked diligently to ensure that every child in her residential nursery was emotionally fueled and became a partner in a reciprocal, attentive, and nurturing relationship. This evolved into a pedagogical system, which included the structure of the institute, creating the right environment, the attitude of the adults, following the individuality and the development of the children. Through personal constancy, where it is always the same small group of adults caring for the same group of children, they come to know the child personally. And it is *this* connection that invites the caregiver to be gentle.

Colleagues from the Pikler-Lóczy Association Hungary[12] working from the Pikler archives found that the system was built up gradually. Some of the elements had always been present, like the stability of care, but the primary caregiver system evolved over time.

Here is an example: Initially, it was the head caregiver of the group (a caregiver who was like the maternal figure of the group); and while she wasn't the main person with the child, she had the biggest responsibility of the group. Later each caregiver was responsible for two or three children in her group, becoming the significant other. This is now a generally accepted practice in many places.

---

12 See GLOSSARY to learn more about this organization.

This special "know-how" evolved to ensure that the children were being cared for with respect. Three years after opening the infants' home (it later developed into an institute where courses continue to be offered in various languages) and putting her ideas in a book (*There Are No Orphans in Socialism,* 1950), Pikler confidently believed that it was possible to raise healthy babies in an institution. This was her goal.

The reason for sharing these ideas is to understand why and how Pikler's ideas worked and why the Institute was set up the way it was. There are many caring individuals and governments that want to improve conditions in institutions. However, while we have seen that priorities that are often placed, for example, on cramming in activities and decorating the environment, *at the Pikler Institute, it was about relationships,* primarily those that offered the child opportunities to bond with a main person who would sustain him emotionally.

Chapter 1.3

There can be no keener revelation of a society's soul than the way in which it treats its children.

—Nelson Mandela

Who Was Emmi Pikler?

The extraordinary woman, wife, mother, and forward-thinking pediatrician, Emmi Pikler, was born Emilie Madleine Reich to Henrich Reich and Hermina on January 9, 1902, in Vienna. Her father was a craftsman, while her mother of Austrian origin was a kindergarten teacher. The family moved to Budapest in 1908, where, six years later, her mother died.

When Pikler was eighteen, she returned to Vienna to begin her university studies, and after graduating, she received her license to practice as a pediatrician in 1930. Pikler had been inspired by, among others, the renowned Austrian pediatrician, Prof. Clemens von Pirquet, as well as by Prof. Hans Salzer, a child surgeon at the Mauthner Markhof Clinic.

Pirquet had emphasized the practical training of his students, as well as his belief that children, whether sick or well, should spend time in fresh air where they could play and move about freely. It was this kind of thinking that enabled Pikler to create an appropriate environment for children to be able to sleep outdoors during their afternoon nap in comfortable and spacious sleeping bags.

From Salzer, Pikler learned that even unpleasant examinations or treatments could be performed without the child's crying, if, that is, he is touched gently. This fundamental principle that infants must always be touched with gentle but definitive movements became a guiding principle for Pikler.

There was also a kind of spirituality brewing in the culture at that time, with many new currents and directions being developed and practiced. It was then that Pikler learned about healthy diets, nutrition, and nature, looking to her sister-in-law, who had healed quickly after undergoing lung surgery while adhering to the philosophy of Elsa Gindler.[13]

Gindler's approach focused on the development of awareness of the senses and to come in contact with oneself. In her sessions, she invited participants to express themselves through conscious posture, movements, and breathing in a natural and authentic manner. Her somatic work also played a key role in the development of body psychotherapy.[14]

Sharing the same belief of being present in the world at large, to what is now commonly known as mindfulness, Pikler then invited Gindler to Budapest. Unable to visit, Gindler instead put her in touch with her disciple Elfriede Hengstenberg.

Hengstenberg and Pikler, together with a group of colleagues and friends, met for four weeks each summer During the years 1935-1937 to experiment with this new way of being. Hengstenberg and Pikler then refocused their energies on children; allowing them to find their equilibrium (emotional and physical) by being offered a safe environment to autonomously explore laws of gravity.

---

13 See Glossary for Elsa Gindler's biography.

14 *"Elsa Gindler and her influence on Wilhelm Reich and Body Psychotherapy"* (2009), Ulfried Geuter, Michael C. Heller and Judyth O. Weaver.

The connection between Pikler and Gindler continues today at the Pikler Institute with the work of Ute Strub, a disciple of Hengstenberg.

These theories helped foster Pikler's notion of returning to nature and, with it, a healthier way of life, one that also adhered to preventing diseases, not only treating them. She incorporated this approach into her practice and developed a complex system of providing care for and bringing up healthy infants and young children under age three.

After meeting György Pikler, a high school mathematics teacher, in Vienna, the couple married in 1930 and then moved to Trieste, Italy. An important element of her husband's pedagogy was that children should follow their own developmental rhythm in their studies. The pediatrician then applied these precepts to her own work.

Together, the couple decided that in raising their child, Anna, born in 1931, they were not going to follow traditional teaching methods but would instead provide the child opportunities for free movement, free playing, and the idea of getting acquainted with the world. These practices allowed Anna to develop in accordance with her own individual pace and rhythm, starting from birth.

In 1935, Pikler became a licensed pediatrician in Hungary, working as a family doctor in Budapest. Her patients were families that chose to follow her then-revolutionary principles of bringing up infants and young children. Regularly visiting families in their own homes, Pikler would then observe the development and behavior of infants in their natural environment.

In the course of these visits, she taught the parents what to notice in their children's behavior and how to recognize and respond to the child's needs. As was the case with her own child, Pikler sought and provided the conditions necessary for independent, self-initiated movement and playing activities. She also taught the parents how to observe the child's activities and discoveries starting from newborn age.

In addition, Pikler instructed these families that to be occupied with their child should neither primarily be characterized by constantly holding and pampering him nor should it consist of "teaching him" (not disturbing his natural development by teaching him how to walk or play, for example.) Above all, this approach to childrearing should mean utilizing the time of care—breastfeeding, feeding, bathing, dressing—as joyful, serene, and peaceful, during which time the infant is an active participant.

The more actively the child was encouraged to participate, Pikler believed, the better for all concerned. Indeed, "Pikler children" were extremely independent: They occupied themselves with their own activities, and they did not continuously demand the presence of their parents, thus allowing the parents more energy for their own tasks.

A circle of families enthusiastic about this educational method slowly formed, while children who grew up this way were proud that they were "Pikler children," even as the rest of the world often regarded what was then considered to be an extremely unusual upbringing. In general, people observed that these children were more "peaceful."

After publishing articles on the topic of bringing up small children, Pikler published her first book in 1940,[15] originally titled *What Can the Baby Already Do?* The book summarized the experiences she had observed with her patients, specifically focusing on free gross motor movement (without teaching or assisting children in how to reach their developmental milestones) and in the healthy growth of children.

However, the ten years that she worked as a family pediatrician were difficult for Pikler, both because her family was Jewish and because her husband had been in prison from 1936 to 1945 for political reasons. During the war years, Pikler and her family were able to survive because some of her patients had not only procured false documents for the Piklers, but hid them as well.

After the war, in 1946, Pikler established an infants' home in a house with a large garden on Lóczy Lajos Street in the Rose Hill

---

15 By putting this question in quotes in the original Hungarian title, Dr. Pikler was addressing the competitive attitude by many parents, expressing their desire to get their children to do things as soon as possible. The title was changed in the German publication to *Peaceful Babies – Contented Mothers.*

neighborhood of Budapest. Here she had the opportunity to test her educational principles within institutional circumstances.

Building on her experience and observations gained in the course of her work with families, Pikler began to lay the foundations for the healthy personality development of children growing up in institutions. This was accomplished by providing the proper caregiver-child relationship, as well as giving the children opportunities to participate in free activities.

In her 1950 book *There Are No Orphans in Socialism*, Pikler summarized the objectives of the institute: "When establishing the Institute, we set it as our goal to raise the infants entrusted to our care, as physically and mentally healthy children that do not display any disadvantage of being institutionalized."

Pikler was convinced that, in applying her principles, the harms of institutional upbringing could be avoided. This was also a test of her methods, with the results of the follow-up studies proving her right. Hence, children in institutions were given an opportunity to avoid the already well-known institutional harm, hospitalism.

The beginnings of the institute were not easy. Soon after opening the home, Pikler decided to dismiss the old-fashioned, trained nurses originally employed as caregivers. They were more keen on keeping order in the cupboards than being respectful with the children. In addition, these women didn't talk to the children, and their movements were quick and impersonal. The result was that the children were treated as objects.

Pikler replaced these nurses with untrained young women who were taught to touch the children gently and to whom she could personally teach the art of care.

Pikler was the director of the infants' home for 32 years, during which time it became an internationally renowned institution, one where further education and trainings directly related to the practical work were also conducted. In 1971, Lóczy also became the National Methodological Center Of Infants' Homes in Hungary.

Generations of early childhood professionals, including the managers of other institutions, caregivers, and other experts, gained exceptional knowledge and career-defining experience from Emmi Pikler.

Beginning in 1977, Pikler also regularly gave lectures abroad, including in most of the European countries and in the United States. This meant that the development of the Piklerian practice and approach that Pikler and her colleagues had worked out were being recognized worldwide: that children raised in institutions can grow up both physically and mentally healthy.

Scientific work was also conducted at the institute in various fields, the most significant of which was research by Pikler that was first published in Hungarian in 1968. In it, Pikler explored the characteristics and the course of free, self-initiated motor development. Her book describing the results of this research, as well as her other books, have since been translated and published in several languages, including German, Slovakian, Spanish, and French.

Pikler headed the institute until 1978, after which time she continued to work there as a scientific fellow. Succeeding Pikler as director was pediatrician Judit Falk, who had worked as Pikler's deputy for many years. Pikler gave her last lecture in 1983 in Berlin, where she talked about the importance of providing opportunities for free movement and free playing to infants. She died in Budapest on June 6, 1984.

Pikler's legacy is preserved, and her work is continued by the Emmi Pikler Daycare Center, Pikler Lóczy Association Hungary, and Lóczy Foundation for Children, operating in the same building in Budapest as the infants' home, which was shut down by the Hungarian government in 2011.

On the global level, there are dozens of Pikler associations and Pikler foundations in several European countries, North and South America, New Zealand, and Australia, as well as the umbrella organization, International Pikler Association, all of which continue to spearhead and champion her ideas.

Chapter 1.4

Presence involves being aware of what is happening as it is happening, being receptive to our own inner mental sea, and attuning to the inner life of another person. Being present for others means we resonate with what is going on in their inner worlds, creating the essential way we feel their feelings.

—Dr. Daniel Siegel, PhD[16]

The following text, delivered by Pikler at a medical conference,[17] recounts how her original experiences as a family pediatrician formed the basis of her ideas in organizing the residential nursery.

OUR ASPIRATIONS AND RESULTS AT THE PIKLER® INSTITUTE, BUDAPEST [18]

By Dr. Emmi Pikler

"The infants' home of our institute, the Lóczy Institute (bearing the name of the street where it is located), started its operation on July 1, 1946. Since then, for over 32 years, nearly 2000[19] children have been raised here.

---

16 Brainstorm, Daniel Siegel, MD, p. 218.

17 Pedagogical, Psychological, Developmental Psychological Medical Conference in Budapest, Hungary, October 25, 1978. The Hungarian Psychological Association and the Hungarian Pediatrician Association.

18 NATIONAL METHODOLOGICAL INSTITUTE OF INFANTS' HOMES, Budapest, II. Lóczy L. u. 3. LECTURES – COMMUNICATIONS DOCUMENTS XXIII 1979, Manuscript. Second Edition/ Lecture 1978, L/216/78.

19 Around 2,500 infants were reared at the Pikler Institute until its closing in 2011.

The gates of Pikler Institute

Since 1970, the National Methodological Institute has been supervising all infants' homes in Hungary and making efforts to improve their work with our professional guidance.

Generally, newborn babies who are only influenced by the education and care they receive at our institute, apart from the neonatal or maternity departments, are accepted. Consequently, our successes and failures are our own; nobody else may be held responsible. It is a serious challenge to raise babies in an institute without families or even the outlines of a relationship model in a way that they could become healthy, balanced, sociable, and moral people.

However, we welcomed this challenge.

In the first years, we mostly dealt with the organization of the practice, the education of proper staff, and the development of the documentary method. When the first few years' results turned out to be satisfactory, we could start processing the material gathered and doing research.

From the very beginning, the Lóczy Institute intended to look after resident babies and infants in a way different from the usual method. The target was to implement the education and care system tried and tested and effective in families for years within an institutional framework.

How is this education and care system different from the system generally accepted then and even now?

In families where the education and care system was exemplary for us, caretaking—contrary to the usual perception—was regarded to be something more than just the means of physical care, and infants were educated not only outside these activities, but also these care periods became the centers of education.

Mothers scheduled their day so that they would have ample time to care for their children, to feed, dress, bathe their infants patiently, taking their time; and in the meantime, they could pick up even the youngest newborns' signals. The mothers were instructed to try establishing good cooperation as soon as possible. They were requested not to hurry, to talk to their babies, to call their attention to the objects they were using, and to what was happening to the infants themselves; they asked the babies' help and waited for their reactions; and they also had to respond to initiatives.

Experience showed that even babies could easily remember and understand what they were expected to do, and they did it, if sufficient time was available and care was given not by overcoming their resistance, but by compassion and response to their signals.

As a result, a routine was established which made understanding each other easier. The relationship between mother and child was so peaceful and calm that both of them could become more self-confident, more secure in each other's company; they got to know and to love each other.

The mother also needs free time for herself and the chores so that she could pay attention to her child with patience, without hurry, and with enough time to spare, so that she could enjoy the time spent together and caring for the infant. Similarly, the children, even babies, need undisturbed, peaceful periods for sleeping or watching their surroundings or hands, for manipulating objects, moving around and playing to their hearts' content.

If the infants' relationship to their mothers is well balanced, they are at ease, looking around, playing even alone without requiring the mother's constant attention. This requires the infant to be provided with proper clothes, sufficient room for movement, suitable toys, and such a routine, which the infant may get accustomed and adapt to.

However, it must be noted that there is another prerequisite for the children's independent movement and play from their earliest age. They must never be or placed in a situation they are unable to get in and leave independently nor may they be fixed in a device (baby chair, baby rocking chair, standee chair, etc.) because that makes them incapacitated, dependent, and helpless without the help of an adult. Experience shows that if children are happy, active, and have enough room to practice various movements, they feel like practicing, and if they are provided with toys they are interested in, they do not need assistance from an adult to learn to change their situation and position: they can turn around, crawl, climb, sit up, stand up, and walk.

Based on the care and education in model families, we could establish that, contrary to the opinion described in a lot of professional literature according to which infants cry and feel insecure without their mothers, infants cared for with attention and patience are happy and well balanced at their play area. They did not feel abandoned if their mothers were doing their chores within earshot and were only available if the children needed help. The infant was calm, peaceful, and developed well, while the mother also had time for other things. She did not need to hurry when looking after her child. She was happy to have her infant in her arms and was happy that they could spend time together during caretaking.

Nowadays, it is generally accepted that the relationship between mother and her very young child is the model for all human relationships. It is during the development of this relationship that the infant learns to love and to get in touch, gets to know and to love the mother, and the mother learns to get to know her child, and her understanding grows together with her love. The child's social inclusion and moral base are established within this relationship.

The development of this relationship is harder if the mother only pays attention to satisfying physical needs and she teaches things she considers important to the child only outside the caregiving time. It is not the most practical way to build the relationship in teaching situations independent from everyday, common, practical tasks. It is in vain if the child learns about lots of things if, emotionally, his or her life is bleak and the basis of moral development was not built in the age when it is possible through appropriate mother-child relationship. This relationship primarily develops during caretaking, in the course of interactive tasks.

Even though this kind of education requires more care, more intensive attention during caretaking, and more careful organization of the environment so that the child would really be and feel secure, mothers happily welcomed and implemented this approach. As for the children, while their relationship became more intense with their mothers, they learned everything they were expected to during their development, on the basis of their own, independent initiatives without having been "taught" according to a plan.

When grown up, these children remember their childhood as a pleasant and happy period of their lives. They also try to educate their own children in a similar manner. What happened to them feels natural. They believe that this is the way to bring up their children to become intelligent, happy people who are able to fit in and love.

This is the education system we wanted to implement at the Lóczy Institute.

Consequently, the focus was on establishing proper quality care within the frame of suitable primary care when the institute was opened.

However, the group of infants and their caregiver must stay unchanged for a considerable period so that the children could be cared for well in the sense described above and so that the infant and the caretaking adult can get to know and get accustomed to each other.

The target is that during the day shift, a group of eight, or maximum nine, infants would be looked after by a very few number of the same adults, if possible. The group of children should stay together, if possible, throughout their entire stay at the institute, and if some leave the institute for good, the newly admitted children would take their places, as opposed to ones from other groups.

This is important because even if the caregiver loves children in general, is able, neat, and experienced, she would not be able to build an intimate relationship with the infant if she does not know the infants she looks after well, if she was working once in this group, then in another group, and if the composition of the group constantly changes.

This would force her to perform the work as a routine, as she could not know the individual signals of each infant, his or her behavior, and neither can the children get to know her. As a result, the children's signals, as well as the caregiver's signals, remain unanswered, and this would lead to fewer signals on both parts and the adults' work becoming more and more mechanical and the children increasingly passive. In this manner, they are unable to get accustomed to each other or create an emotional human bond.

The caregiver, no matter how able and gentle, would remain just an indifferent adult, one out of many, who does not cause unnecessary pain during caretaking at best. They would be living peacefully side by side.

Therefore, the personal relationship essential for the social development of the child can only develop if the group of children and the caregiver team are constant. This has been our target at the Lóczy Institute from the very beginning. Its implementation may seem simple, but in fact, this proves to be a serious organizational challenge to the director of the institution. The same was experienced at infants' homes, which, after taking our advice, have attempted to organize permanent groups with caregivers in recent years.

The caregiver can only look after children in a continuous and calm manner if, similarly to the family model, other children play and move actively (if not asleep) while she pays attention to one child. Spacious play areas must be provided so that several children can play at the same time without disturbing one another.

The stages of motor development in the family model were of exceptional importance for children living in groups. If given proper space, children do not need the direct assistance of an adult to learn gross motor skills. If they can and do feel like moving around independently, they become able to reach their toys alone, manipulate them and play with them, and take in their hands whatever they like and are interested in. In this way, the shared play area becomes a hive of activity that the caregiver keeps an eye on but her permanent help is not required.

Since one caregiver must look after eight to nine children, obviously, there cannot be as much time spent with the care of each child as the mother has for her own child. Nevertheless, our experience shows that if the quality of care is good and the caregivers do not change, it is possible to see that infants are active and play happily alone, that they do not cry to be cared for out of turn, even inside the institute. Naturally, the caregiver stays in touch with them in their play area, talks to them, and if she picks up one child, addresses the others too, responds when called for, and provides assistance if she sees that a child needs help. If play areas are roomy enough and children's groups are constant, even infants seem to find some compensation in playing among the others rather than alone.

This was the basic idea, the concept, and the practice behind the work started in the Lóczy Institute. We wanted to achieve the children's approximately normal development, that they would not only learn what children of their age need to know, but also that their emotional life and related skills would develop, active social integration would commence, and a sound basis for their moral development would be provided.

I have discussed infants' care in detail primarily. We believe that this is the time during which our results are established. Needless to say, in the case of older children, of ages one and half to three, education gains ground outside caretaking tasks. Even then, the significance of education based on cooperation with the child and on mutual understanding offered during the satisfaction of physical needs does not diminish during the three-year stay at the institute.

The development of children was as expected during the time they spent at the institute. Infants are generally happy and active, their physical development is satisfactory, and their relationship with their caregiver is intimate and affectionate. Their good physical and mental status is also reflected in the low number of illnesses.

Even though we could be satisfied, we were primarily interested in the major problems of children raised in the institute, their later development and social inclusion. The most important question is, how they cope in a family? It is all the more important, since it was their adverse social conditions that originally necessitated their placement at the institution.

For this reason, we have conducted follow-up examinations.

The first follow-up was performed in 1968 and supported by the World Health Organization (WHO). We located 168 former residents who spent at least their first year of life at our institute and then were raised in families, to the best of our knowledge. In 1968, they were between 13 and 22 years old. The data of those 100 young people who agreed to the psychological examination were processed. We could be satisfied with the results.

Of all the difficulties related to the lack of will and initiative, to the deficiencies of establishing contact, which hit those children the hardest who spent the first years of their lives at an institute, we did not experience any with our children. They could integrate in society, their formal education was somewhat better that that of the average; five of the women had already had babies, all of them of married, and they were all looking after their own children. No criminal activity occurred.

Our children did not prove to be exceptionally gifted; they were all of average intelligence. We were really happy with this, as we are convinced that even the best infants' home cannot provide as much as a loving mother in an average, normal family.

In 1978, we contacted and/or contacted again the children participating in the 1968 examination to find out if and how they managed later on. They are 24 to 33 years old. The examination is still in progress. Out of the 100 children, 96 could be found and 90 were interviewed. The picture is more complex than in 1968.

Generally speaking, the children have adapted well, though the life of some is not really favorable. As for their formal education, only one out of the 90 did not finish elementary school, and 27 of them, i.e., approximately one third, graduated from or are still attending college or university. They have a total of 63 children, who are all raised in their own families.

As for the scientific and methodological work of our institute, I would like to give a basic outline of what we have been dealing with for 32 years. We have tackled the organizational and construction problems of infants' homes, their internal organizational issues, the elaboration of specific job descriptions, and arranging the children's future. We have been providing further professional trainings, which are assisted by 11 training materials on films recorded at our institute and marketed in several languages. We have created a chart to continuously control the development of children below three years of age.

We have been dealing with motor development, the development of manipulation, social skills, and speech, with the proper manner of providing assistance to infants' gathering experiences, with the building and conditions of adult-child relationship. Our scientific and promotional materials have been published both in and outside Hungary.

Before finishing my lecture, I would like to add that it is an exceptionally exciting opportunity to observe the development of children raised at our institute. The extraordinary circumstances we organized enable us to observe such development potentials and processes that could not be created in another system. It is very complex work to observe, accurately register the development, clarify its circumstances, and explore the influence of the environment. This is hard work, and this is how we try to illuminate some issues related to infant care and education."

The Pikler® Pedagogy in Today's World

Even though the aforementioned article is nearly 40 years old, the principles and their applications are still relevant. Indeed, the Pikler pedagogy—bringing up infants and young children with respect—continues to be practiced throughout the world by parents and professionals. Wherever Dr. Emmi Pikler's approach is practiced, a significant improvement in the quality of life of infants and young children and the adults who care for them occurs.

Thanks to the dedicated efforts carried out by the different Pikler associations worldwide, Pikler's principles are not only being applied in institutions, but also in family settings, as well as being studied and taught at the university level.

Since Pikler's death in 1984, thousands of participants from around the globe have attended one-week trainings onsite at the Pikler Institute (over 200 students per year), and thousands more have conducted observations at both the Pikler infants' home and the Pikler Daycare Center. Certified Pikler trainers also offer trainings in various countries.

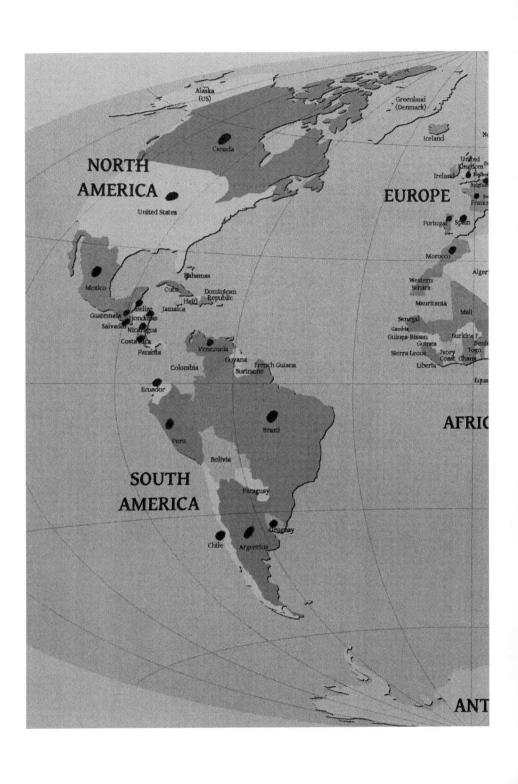

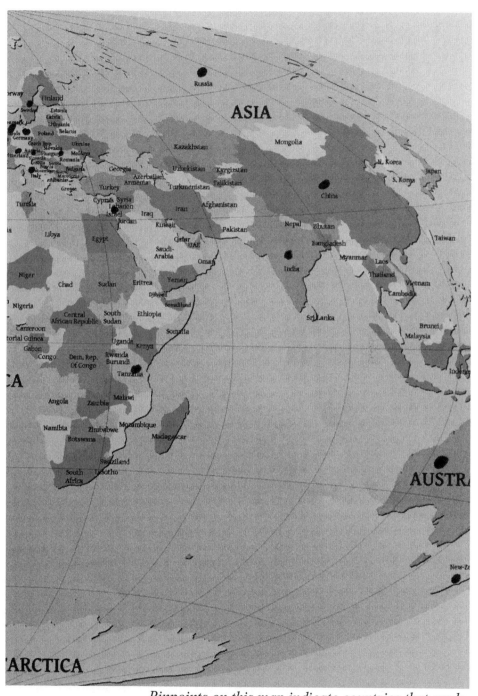

Pinpoints on this map indicate countries that apply the principles of the Pikler pedagogy.

In addition, there are also a number of books[20] and programs that have been inspired by the Pikler pedagogy. It is safe to say then that Dr. Emmi Pikler and her unique approach to childrearing has made an impact on thousands of students and professionals worldwide.

Testimonials from Around the World:

Emmi Pikler was one of the great educators of the 20th century, and I believe we have yet to fully consider all the consequences and implications of her vision of early childhood development. A pioneer in her approach, she was first and foremost a great observer of the mental growth and maturation of children growing up at home – as a pediatrician, she visited families and helped parents to respect the individual development pace of each child and to put in place the possibilities of free motricity (free activity), i.e. their freedom of physical movement, which is an essential condition for freedom of mental movement, i.e. their future freedom of thought.

The end of World War II left Pikler shocked – as a pediatrician, as a woman and, quite simply, as a human being – by the suffering of the youngest children roaming through the rubble of what was left of Budapest (children later referred to as "survivors of the tempest"). Thus, she founded the nursery of Loczy Street, where, between 1946 and 2011, almost 5,000 infants and toddlers under the age of 6 were fostered.

Given the difficulty of caring for children about whom hardly anything was known, an exceptional professionalization of the care given to those young children was created and implemented at the Loczy Institute – based on the principles which characterize the so-called Pikler Approach, subject of this work.

I would say one of Emmi Pikler's first key ideas was the founding of this nursery, emphasizing from the outset that the aim was not just to let the hosted children survive physically (which in itself would already have been legitimatization enough!), but to also enable them, in spite of everything, to develop mentally as persons worthy of

---

20 See references for a partial listing of books that have been inspired in the Pikler pedagogy.

that denomination, i.e. persons who would not only be respected by others, but who would also be able to respect themselves.

This is a veritable life lesson one cannot but admire. Hence, the work of Emmi Pikler is genuinely revolutionary for at least three reasons:

First of all, the Pikler Approach is fundamentally rooted in observation and facts, which makes it a core principle, as children can only develop in a harmonious way when they are carefully observed by the adults caring for them.

Observation is therefore both means of Piklerian understanding and tool of its impact on children, making it a kind of permanent action research, cutting edge in the field of epistemology.

What's more, the human newborn showing a significantly higher neoteny (physiological immaturity) in physical, neurological and mental terms compared to all other mammals, the Pikler Approach nonetheless values the potential competences of the infant who, despite this neoteny, can and should be co-actor in his or her own development.

There is clearly a great functional asymmetry between the human adult and the human infant; however, there is also the possibility of reciprocity and mutuality between them from the beginning, which announced, in a brilliant way, the famous "fundamental anthropological situation", later theorized in the works of Jean Laplanche[21].

Lastly, even though the Pikler ethic is based on the fact that the quality of early childhood care appears as a categorical imperative, intrinsically justified as such, without the need for any further legitimization from other fields, today's spectacular advancements in neuroscience do, as it were – more than 50 years after her original work – come to confirm Emmi Pikler's revolutionary clinical intuitions – and that in several important domains, like multisensory synchrony, access to intersubjectivity, maturative effects of free activity.

This is what I strived to show in an article published some time ago on the Pikler International website, in order to underline the genuinely innovative dimension of the Pikler Approach

---

21   Jean Lapanche (1924-2012) was a French psychoanalyst and author of "The Language of Psycho-Analysis" (Lapanche, Pontalis), 1974.

In his film produced for the occasion of the Loczy nursery's closing, Bernard Martino[22] describes the Pikler Approach as a "school of civilization", and I believe he is perfectly right. Certainly, Emmi Pikler's works concern, first and foremost, children living in institutions (thus the importance of this publication by Elsa Chahin and Anna Tardos), but in reality they concern all children, to the extent that all children go through a first period of great dependence on their environment, during which it is crucial to help them be active and progressively discover their own resources, in order to let them enjoy the power of turning their competences into performances all by themselves. Even today, this new way of understanding early development remains revolutionary, for, despite being rooted in clinics and the results from observation, it remains an object of resistance, insofar as adults are always more or less ambivalent towards their own childhood, facing the child they used to be or fear to have been.

A special thanks to Elsa Chahin and Anna Tardos for reminding us with such intellect and profoundness of the fundamental rights of children in institutional care, i.e. ultimately the fundamental needs of development in general – needs so well understood and ensured by the Pikler® Approach.
—France-based Dr. Bernard Golse[23]

A worldwide challenge to rearing infants and toddlers in institutions is to come up with methods that create whole, healthy, functioning children who can operate inside and outside institutional settings.

---

22 Bernard Martino is a French filmmaker. Films include "Lóczy, A Place to Grow" (2000), and *"Lóczy, A School of Civilization"* (2014).

23 Dr. Bernard Golse, pediatric psychiatrist-psychoanalyst and Head of the Pediatric Psychiatry division at the *Hôpital Necker – Enfants Malades* [Children's hospital] in Paris, and director of the French division of the World Association for Infant Mental Health. See CONTRIBUTORS section for his biography.

The Pikler Institute has met that challenge by working out a carefully planned and tested approach over the last six decades.
– Janet Gonzalez-Mena, author of *"Infants, Toddlers, and Caregivers: A Curriculum of Respectful, Responsive, Relationship-Based Care and Education".*

The application of the Pikler Pedagogy in orphanages in Nicaragua has offered caregivers the possibility to establish real relationships with the children under their care, opening channels for a more respectful and close communication between them. Eleven years after implementing Pikler's ideas of care in the centers in Nicaragua, the positive impact on children is noticeable and enduring, not only in themselves but also with the people who have just entered their lives. As is the case with adoptive parents, knowing about the quality of care that had been provided to their children, they are grateful and confident that this is not something that remains as a childhood experience but an experience for the rest of their lives.—**El Salvador-based Tamara Bayres Mosher, psychologist**

After visiting the Pikler residential nursery, I want to reiterate how impressed I was by the warm and respectful method this institution employs with children. I am convinced that implementing this system and its techniques for child development—based on respect as persons and individuals—in Mexican childcare institutions, will bear great results so that children, who do not have the privilege of a traditional and stable family, can grow with respect and love toward their neighbors and society as a whole. I delight in the interest that Pikler's work has gained in Mexico and other countries.
—**His Excellency José Luis Martinez Hernandez, Mexico's former Ambassador to Hungary**

Emmi Pikler's work has had a huge impact on the lives of children, families, and educators in New Zealand, and is also gaining traction in Australia, with educators and parents who work with very young children.
—**Melbourne-based Katherine Bussey, M.Ed**

Observing at Lóczy was the inspiration behind my decision to research diapering practices in a Midwest U.S. city. Lóczy exemplifies an approach with children based on child readiness rather than school readiness. Research about diapering in U.S. infant and toddler settings is overlooked in the literature, especially about the caregiver-child relationship. By shedding light on diapering routines—through small steps and small changes—current diapering practices could be transformed as a source of joy for both caregiver and child. The moment-to-moment experiences in care routines are significant anchored moments between a child and a caregiver in their day.
—Deborah Laurin, PhD candidate and researcher from Canada

Knowing Emmi Pikler's vision of childhood has helped me to not only connect with parents, but also to convey to them the great importance of the first years of a child's life.
—Mexico-based Raquel Puga, psychologist

Dr. Emmi Pikler's work is timeless because the offering of deep respect to another person is universal, and everlasting. Dr. Pikler's gift to all humanity was having the completeness of mind to offer the depth, and breadth, of one's respect to the most vulnerable among us: The young child. Her pedagogy, developed over her many years of service, working and being with abandoned infants, takes the simplest of interactions with children, and gives it meaning through a shared connection of the moment. I can't think of a better knowledge, than to learn to develop this shared connection in the way that Dr. Pikler, her colleagues and her students have demonstrated. This book makes clear Dr. Pikler's life-fulfilling, life-confirming and life-sustaining methodology – one of the most essential works of our time.
—New York-based Harold Rosenthal, Early Childhood Specialist at the Institute for Infants Children and Families of the Jewish Board of Family and Children's Services.

Through Pikler's work, I have learned to communicate with young children and respect their individual essence and personal space.

Pikler's philosophy offers a deep understanding of the importance of love, acceptance and respect... of how every caregiving interaction becomes a mutual exchange to learn from one another. The seeds of her work bear fruit to the great human qualities inherent in all of us.
—**Morocco-based Elke Bardor, mother, volunteer and philanthropist**

As a parent and someone who works with parents and children, the work of Dr. Pikler and her mentee Magda Gerber continues to inspire me daily. Living in a fast-paced Singapore, I am reminded to observe, slow down, and be in partnership with my children. I thank you for continuing the work of Dr. Pikler. May her legacy continue to inspire many others.
—**Singapore-based Shumei Winstaneley, cofounder of Chapter Zero Singapore**

I am awed by the fact that a woman, a pediatrician, so many years ago, when there were no computers to look up data, spent many long precious hours collecting such important information about babies and toddlers.
—**Israel-based Miriam Blau, educational day-care counselor**

I created Juego y Crianza *to offer young children a safe space where they can play autonomously as protagonists of their own initiatives, without needing an adult's direct intervention. Based on the Pikler's principles of free movement and spontaneous play, the environment is set up with developmentally appropriate objects and structures that invite children to explore with curiosity and focused attention; with parents respecting their unique rhythm, and enjoying their process.*
—**Argentina-based Vanesa Valle, early childhood specialist**

Dr. Pikler's approach has opened important doors for children and their families and has been completely transcendental for me and for the children I have worked with.
—**Puerto Rico-based Elsa Arenas, Waldorf educator from Columbia**

As a facilitator of Pikler trainings for professionals, I witness every day how the participants are filled with awe and wonder at the discoveries they are making about the children they engage with. In this age of misunderstanding and discontent, there is nothing more important than how we are with the children. Give them their freedom from the start and they will blossom and unfold to become the adults the world needs.

—United Kingdom-based Rachel Tapping, parent-and-child group leader

To accompany children's development with sincere respect, trust and acceptance, results in much more than mere companionship. Imagine if all children grew up to become authentic, learning from their own selves and from others; imagine what world we would be creating. A child will treat others as he/she has been treated. For that reason, we need to let Emmi Pikler's ideas be known all over the world, in each school, in each orphanage, in each family, in every corner.

—Spain-based Ane Garmendia, early childhood educator, and Pikler® pedagogue candidate

The continued work and research of Dr. Emmi Pikler is as important today as the day she began in Hungary. All children everywhere deserve respect and to be valued as she so eloquently described over and over through her research. My life is changed because of it, and so are the people I come in contact with—caregivers, teachers, and educators—and the hundreds of children who have passed though our school and family child care.

—United States of America-based Roseann Murphy, early childhood education consultant

After reading about Dr. Pikler, I wanted to apply these principles with my own baby. I am extremely thankful for all the knowledge that I was able to quickly absorb. Now that my son is five months old, I can already see how Dr. Pikler's teachings have literally changed my family's life.

—**Mexico-based Amanda Kennedy, a new mother**

It is through Pikler's ideas that I am able to give the best that I have to offer to the young children with whom I have the honor of sharing the joy of being together.

—**Costa Rica-based Sary Montero, lead caregiver**

PART TWO

At the center of nonviolence stands the principle of love.

—Martin Luther King, Jr.

Declaration of the Rights of Young Children[24] Living in Children's Homes

Submitted by the Working Group of the Pikler/Lóczy Association Hungary [25]

All children living in institutions have the right to be highly valued as group members and also as individuals in order that they can experience a complete (developmentally and emotionally sound) childhood throughout their stay.

In order to achieve this we declare the following rights to be essential:

1. All children living in institutions have the right to a healthy life in all its aspects: nutritious food, appropriate clothing, clean environments, and fresh air. In other words, they have the right to physical well-being and good health.
2. All children have the right to develop an individual, personal, loving, and supportive relationship with the adults who take care of them. These adults must know them well so they can take their individual, physical and emotional needs into consideration.
3. All children have the right to be treated as individuals so that their physical and psychological needs are met; they are not hurried, and they end up being satisfied and have their own personal belongings.[26]
4. All children have the right to be protected from all types of aggression, open or hidden, verbal, emotional or physical, and

---

24 For our purposes, we are referring to young children between zero and three, the most critical and sensitive years in the life of a child.

25 Edited by Janet Gonzalez Mena

26 Addition of personal belongings submitted by Dr. Oleg Palmov, associate professor, Department of Mental Health and Early Childhood Intervention, Faculty of Psychology, St. Petersburg State University.

have the right to experience the acceptance and respect every human being is entitled to.

5. All children have the right to continuity and stability in their personal relationships, physical environment, and life circumstances, including a predictable organization of events in their everyday lives.

6. All children should be able to satisfy their natural need for activity, to have the possibility of moving and playing freely, discovering their surroundings and developing their capacities.

7. All children have the right to be able to create a positive image of themselves.

8. All children have the right to get support and respect for their individual rhythm of development.

9. All children have the right to know their personal history and to get support to stay in contact with their families.[27]

10. All children should have the right to be helped in finding a beneficial solution to live in a loving family.

*When the declaration of the *Ten Rights for Young Children Living in Children's Homes* was drafted, the idea of having these ten points was later developed and evolved to satisfy the needs of children living in families and attending day care.

This gave birth to the declaration of the *Ten Rights of Children Attending a Daycare Center.* There is an obvious difference between these two declarations. In the rights for children living in children's homes, there are two points that have to do with family. However, in the rights for children attending a day-care center, there is only one right that refers to family:

Family is the nucleus and community of the child and must be respected at the day-care center.

---

27   Addition of personal history submitted by Dr. Oleg Palmov.

Chapter 2.1

The Right to a Healthy Life

All children living in institutions have the right to a healthy life in all of its aspects: nutritious food, appropriate clothing, personal belongings, clean environments, and fresh air. In other words, they have the right to physical well-being and good health.

Nutrition

Our vulnerable children growing up in institutions may come from chaotic beginnings. We want to offer them an opportunity for dignity while nourishing their physical and emotional bodies, whereby they can, in turn, feel good about themselves.

There is a harsh reality to take into account when considering the right to nutritious food. Many impoverished nations are not able to offer proper nutrition. Nonetheless, we consider this right essential because it is indeed a right for all children to have access to proper nutrition. We would like to believe that the solution may not be far away and that our advocacy may bring awareness to this crucial need.

It is of utmost importance then to provide a balanced diet rich in nutrients, including carbohydrates, proteins, fats, vitamins, and minerals, as calories ingested in the early years go to not only nourishing the body, but the brain as well. (Mother's breast milk is very important but, unfortunately, is rarely available in institutions.) These nutrients, absorbed by the body and the brain, will support children's ability to grow up healthily, be active, and learn.

A history of poor eating and a dearth of physical activity patterns have a cumulative effect and have contributed to significant nutrition and health challenges that are now faced by much of the world's population. Children who eat nutritious food are more likely to develop well physically and emotionally (positive self-esteem, for example), while issues such as malnutrition and iron-deficiency anemia are less likely to occur.

It is not just about the "what" but also about the "how." Along with the importance of nutritious food that the infant or young child will receive during his stay at the children's home, we add to this the importance on *how* the food is provided to the infants, as feeding is indeed pivotal in building relationships between adult and child.

We do not advocate for the *self-demand* system of feeding in an institution, as it would be impossible for the caregiver to feed every child at his desired time. This would also create chaos. Would only the children that had the will to express their hunger be immediately fed? What would happen to the quieter children who are unable to voice their hunger? Would they not be fed as frequently?

For this reason, we have a proven system that works. It is possible in an institutional setting to create a feeding order for infants that are still fed individually. With a predictable and stable order, caregivers are present to and for each child. The constant routine offers children an opportunity to become aware of their place within the order of the group. Children come to learn that their needs and those of their peers will be met. This predictability, in turn, helps the child build trust in the adult.

We are aware that it may be impossible for each child to be consistently fed by the same adult every time. However, we recommend no more than three or four alternating caregivers during the child's years at the institute. When all the caregivers in the institute are trained on how to care for the children in the same manner, their movements become a conduit for consistency and anticipation.

Feeding time at the Pikler Institute. Photo by Marian Reismann from the Pikler archives.

Eliciting cooperation during feeding time at the Pikler Institute.
Photo by Marian Reismann from the Pikler archives.

They will hold each child in a similar way and offer the spoon or cup also in a similar manner. It will be the child's rhythm that dictates when he's ready for another spoonful or sip, and the caregiver adapts to this flow. By being attentive to the cues, the caregiver will come to know when he is finished and stop the feeding at his slightest indication. The two feeding principles carried out at the Pikler Institute are that new foods are always introduced gradually and that there should never be a spoonful more than what the child wants.

Even as a young infant, the caregivers will hold him in a way where both his arms are able to move freely, thus inviting cooperation when he is ready to help in holding the bottle or cup. The food provided must be in reference to his level of development.

It is important for the child to have his personal preferences taken into consideration by his three or four caregivers. These include the temperature and size of each morsel, disposition to hold spoon or cup, and the pleasure of unhurried time together.

There is a danger of poor feeding that must be pointed out and has to do in great part in our feeding methods. Because independent eating is key for integration into society, it is up to the adult to guide children down this path, never with force or aggression, but with an invitation for a pleasurable relationship with another during the feeding time.

We are aware that what we write about may not always be so simple to implement, as we cannot prescribe a choreography of movements, but we can, however, invite you to set the atmosphere.

The caregiver that knows the child well will come to learn his eating habits and provide joyful opportunities during the feeding. It is not possible for a caregiver who is not familiar to the child and who is not mindful of his individual needs to offer such joy.

As we can see in the following photo, Tünde is replicating with her doll the respectful care she was accustomed to receiving from her caregivers during her feedings.

Tünde at the Pikler Institute when she was a little girl. Photo from the archives of the Pikler Institute.

Researching this book, we had the wonderful opportunity of meeting with Tünde Kertész, the little girl from the photo. Now 25 years old, she has become an early childhood specialist. Having completed her internship at the Pikler Institute, she is currently working as a kindergarten teacher in Budapest, Hungary.

When her lead caregiver (who, at Lóczy, was called the head nurse) received the Emmi Pikler Award in 2016 for her tireless and loving dedication at Lóczy, Tünde attended the ceremony and gave the following speech:

I am happy to be here. Not all of you know this, but I lived here in Lóczy from two months to six years of age. Especially in the last few years, after completing my studies and deciding to become an infant and toddler caregiver, I have realized how proud I am of having had the opportunity to live at Lóczy and to have been able to come back to do my internship here.

Regarding Ms. Marti, the feeling still lingers in me of how much I looked forward to visiting her in the head nurse's room, spending time together, and having a conversation, tête-à-tête, just the two of us. Aside from making drawings with her, I have faded memories, but I know, for sure, how much I loved going to visit her. In fact, she was like a grandmother to me.

We will add more about our conversation with Tünde Kertész in Right 10.

Clothing

As babies begin to interact with their environment and develop their mobility, it is imperative that we complement their natural ability to move freely by providing appropriate clothing. Clothes should be comfortable and provide necessary warmth or coolness, according to the changing seasons, giving infants and young children an opportunity to carry on with their exploration of the environment and activities.

One way of showing our respect to young children is by letting them know that we value their individual level of motor development as well as their comfort level. Dr. Pikler designed the children's clothes in order to support their movement, gross motor development, and adapt to the changing seasons.

What is important here is to think of the child's free movement when dressing him. A practical example is to avoid buttons on the back of his body. A baby should feel at ease when lying supine. We recommend supple fabrics that support elasticity of joints.

Babies do not need shoes when exploring a safe environment. Bare feet offer advantages to mobile infants learning how to crawl or walk. Because he can come to know his own feet as he starts walking, he can move flexibly with his soles. If weather is cold, socks with nonskid soles or soft leather moccasins provide reliable traction. Dresses and skirts can easily interfere with a crawling baby's natural ability to move, as knees can get caught in the fabric.

It is our responsibility to support babies' freedom to move with the appropriate clothing, and the invitation to feel pleasure in the discovery of his locomotion, never by hindering his motor development that would impede him from finding his own balance.

For children growing up in institutions, it is important that they have their "own" clothes, even if it is only one or several items. This will provide a sense of ownership that, in turn, is related to the building of their self-esteem. (See "Personal Belongings" on **chapter 2.3** for more information on this topic.)

Access to Nature and the Outdoors

Safety comes first. When we recommend outdoor time during the day, we want to stress the importance that the children are physically safe, first and foremost. There should always be adult supervision and careful thought invested, so children are away from any danger imposed by nature (climate, flora, or fauna). It would be ideal if the space where children sleep indoors could have direct access to the outdoors. And during their afternoon naps, it is ideal to have a space for their cribs where they are protected from direct sunlight, rain, or snow.

Because of Pirquet's influence on the important aspect of allowing children to spend as much time outdoors as possible (weather permitting), Dr. Pikler first made structural and design changes to the residential nursery. She made sure that every room had direct access to the garden because, if there were stairs, it would be more difficult and take time away from the playtime.

It is good when daytime play is complemented with outdoor play. For young children, this should be in a safe and prepared environment. If all conditions were adequate, babies and children would not only play outdoors during the day, but also have their afternoon naps— both *en plein air*. Dr. Pikler observed that children sleep extremely well outdoors.

The idea is to offer children an opportunity to spend as much time outdoors during the day as possible: to be allowed to not only visit the outdoors, but also to sleep outdoors, play outdoors, and *live* outdoors. This means having all the necessary material conditions available, including toys, cribs, a changing table, a potty, etc. In addition, we also recommend, as part of the daily routine, offering a meal and something to drink in this area.

Outdoor group mealtime at the Pikler Institute. Photo by Marian
Reismann from the Pikler archives.

When Dr. Pikler oversaw all other residential nurseries in
Hungary, many were housed in old castles with large gardens that
resembled parks. She was surprised to find that the outdoor space
was not being used at all and soon implemented her ideas and made
the necessary changes. Children's emotional and physical well-being
improved.

If there are three groups of children in the home, each group
could take one portion of the garden per year. This would mean
that during their first three years of life, each group would enjoy a
different area of the garden.

Outdoor play at the Pikler Institute. Photo by Marian Reismann from the Pikler archives.

A caregiver with children during their outdoor play at the Pikler
Institute. Photo by Marian Reismann from the Pikler archives.

Here is an excerpt from an article written by Dr. Mária Vincze:[28]

"Children's senses work more sharply than ours—they are sharpened for sound, tastes, smells, and sights. When a child encounters nature, he notices the birds singing and the dogs barking from far away. He follows the marching of ants or other insects with concentrated attention. He senses the warmth of the sun on his skin and discovers his shadow.

By moving his hand or altering his position, he observes how it grows, flattens, or changes its shape. He gets acquainted with the elements: runs sands through his fingers, approaches the water on the basin cautiously, only to play with it more pleasurably later on. He learns the difference of how to walk on grass and on stones.

Throughout his entire life, a child never has as many opportunities to sense beauty, discover, experiment, and play in the garden as he does during his first years of life.

This is even more applicable for children growing up in infants' homes.

In order for children to have a truly pleasurable experience and not just an inconsequential moment of hanging about, the garden must be well arranged and equipped. It must be suitable for the children to move freely in it, without the caregiver hindering or limiting their playful mood with constant prohibitions.

The garden is the everyday living space for the children. It is not a destination or an excursion. Neither is it a recreation area nor an amusement park. Therefore, a well-defined part of the garden is just as much a part of the undisturbed group life as is their room inside the house.

In a common garden, without separations for the different groups, the large number of children and the simultaneous presence of several caregivers would disturb the intimate atmosphere.

---

28 Mária Vincze, *The Children's Garden*. Emmi Pikler Public Foundation.

The garden should be child-scaled, neither too large nor too small. If too large, the children will get lost in it, and the caregiver will not know where each child is at any given time. If too small, it loses its magic of discovery, diversity, and spaciousness: four hundred to 500 square feet for the younger ones (one and a half to two years old) and 500 to 800 square feet for the older ones (over two years old).

The occasional natural division of the garden can also be used for separating one section from another. If there is no natural division, then we should artificially plant some dense hedgerow. Sections separated only by fences create a cage-like atmosphere, especially if the garden sections are small.

Slopes, hills, and bumps make the garden versatile. Unevenness should not be evened out. The garden, however, should also have a horizontal part where it is suitable for caregiving activities.

The children should be safe in the garden. A fence that is impenetrable by the children should circle the entire area of the infants' home. It should also be made up of vertical bars, curving inward at the top end, with a gate that must be kept locked.

In the garden of a group of eight children, we need at least one sandpit of six by six feet or two smaller ones of four and a half by four and a half feet. The sandpit should be placed in the area of the garden receiving direct sunlight so that the morning sun can dry out the sand.

We should enable nature to provide the primary experience with its richness. In order for the garden to be really great, for it to live in the memory and dreams of the children, we have to design and organize every detail of the garden life."

There is an interesting anecdote that was experienced by one of Dr. Pikler's patients in the 1930s before she established the nursery home. Pikler had recommended that babies and young children sleep outdoors during their daytime nap, and the families under her care agreed.

One family lived on the second floor of an apartment complex that surrounded a central courtyard. Their only outdoor space was the balcony that connected the apartments with one another. Following Dr. Pikler's recommendation, Mom set the crib "outdoors," which, in her case, was by her front door on the balcony, and proceeded to put her baby down for her afternoon nap.

A neighbor walking by called the superintendent and reported this issue to the police. She reported a case of child endangerment because the weather at that time was quite chilly.

The police arrived and found the child wrapped in a warm sleeping bag, a beanie cap, a blanket, and sleeping peacefully. The policeman saw that the baby was fine and proceeded to inform the neighbors that the child was in no danger whatsoever and let the child continue with his outdoor nap.

This anecdote shows how some people were shocked with Pikler's approach in the beginning, but after observing the results, even skeptics were convinced of her theories.

When the Pikler Daycare Center opened its doors in 2006, there was a discussion of whether to have the children nap outdoors because parents might object. They all agreed it was okay, however, and ultimately gave their consent.

Accompanied Outings

For children that can walk securely [18 months and up], it is recommended that they take walks around their neighborhood or village (reiterating the importance of protection from any harm or danger), accompanied by a caregiver or pedagogue. Ideally, no more than three children per caregiver; if there were more children, the caregiver would only be preoccupied with the children's safety, keeping them in line, for example, instead of enjoying the journey together.

By having a small group per outing, they can all stop from time to time to discuss what they are seeing. These simple, short weekly walks offer the child an opportunity for discovery: to greet others if encountered, to stop and admire a flower if he chooses, and to foster his relationship with the caregiver. Children also gain direct experience about the world that stems beyond his group of peers.

Going for a walk with a caregiver outside the Pikler Institute. Photo by Marian Reismann from the Pikler archives.

Making discoveries during a walk outside the Pikler Institute. Photo by Marian Reismann from the Pikler archives.

Children admiring whatever catches their interest outside the Pikler Institute. Photo by Marian Reismann from the Pikler archives.

Walking back from the outing is also of value. As the children return home, they have a sense of belonging. A child gets to know that the place where he lives is his home. Through this simple yet rich activity of going for a walk and returning home, a child is able greet the head nurse, greet the cook, and also his peers.

Similarly to a child growing up in a family, his world broadens and the walk offers an experience: *"I am not at home because I am walking . . ."* As he returns, he is thinking, *"And now I am at home."*

These outings can serve as preparation for when they are old enough to attend kindergarten or elementary school (in the case that schooling is not provided on site), and the outside world will begin to seem a familiar place, as well as helping him thrive with confidence. Soon enough, they will come to know the world that surrounds them.

In addition to their weekly walks, the children living at the Pikler Institute also enjoyed occasional group excursions, where all the groups and all the caregivers participated.

Children and caregiver from the Pikler Institute on an excursion.
Photo by Marian Reismann from the Pikler archives.

Chapter 2.2

The Right to Stable, Personal, and Loving Relationships

All children have the right to develop an individual, personal, loving, and supportive relationship with the adults who take care of them. These adults must know them well so they can take their individual physical and emotional needs into consideration.

Physical needs and emotional needs are vital, as basic care is not enough. A baby needs more than that: *He must be considered a person.* Because this young baby cannot speak, he may cry to catch the adult's attention, hoping that she interprets these signals as an invitation to slow down, to engage.

Most of the time an adult doesn't mean to be rough in her manner of caring; she simply fails to read any cues emanating from his tense body. Yet something is happening inside this baby's brain. He is forming an image of the world. He is creating synapses; he is adapting to this care, or lack thereof, and deducing that the world is a place where his emotional needs do or do not matter. And he grows according to his experience.

Dr. Pikler suggests that every time an adult has an interaction with a child, she has the opportunity to speak to him, to address him, and to let him know that he matters; that she is there for him, that she is present, available, and accepting of him. She observed that the adult's gestures are imperative in creating a dialogue between her and the baby.

Her voice addresses the infant, and she talks directly to him, not over him. There are questions and answers. Her patient and attentive hands are asking, *"Are you ready for me? Can I pick you up now?"* And the child responds. His body is relaxed, and the tension dissipates. There is a moment of communion between the two, and both are open and receptive to each other.

The infant is being given the opportunity to cooperate, and the adult sees his competence. Such a meaningful and rich encounter can take place because of an organized daily routine.

This togetherness allows the child to accept the world as a trusting place. There is a connection between the adult and the child. It is likely that because both are enjoying the process, they will be yearning for their next encounter: the next bath, the next diaper change. There will be more than basic care being provided, and the baby's emotional needs will be fueled.

But what happens if children's homes consist mostly of volunteers, and every day or perhaps during every meal, the child experiences a new face, a new way of being held, as well as a new manner of speaking? How can the child learn predictability? How can he learn to trust that he matters to someone?

When the child's emotional needs are taken into account and he is embraced as an active participant during all care situations and not just as a passive recipient, this will offer an opportunity for genuine dialogue.

Meaning of Cooperation During Care

In order for the child to prepare for cooperation, he must first feel like he is indeed a participant in his care. The caregiver offers verbal and nonverbal cues regarding what is about to happen and then wait for a response, sensing if the child is ready before executing an action, i.e., picking him up or dressing him. The child's gestures inform the attentive caregiver that he is ready. The togetherness that unfolds increasingly invites the child to take part in an active collaboration. We must then permanently continue to foster a reciprocal atmosphere.

The joy that is shared during the moments of care allow the child to experience spontaneous playfulness. The child may turn his attention to something that catches his interest, and the attentive caregiver may engage by saying, *"These are my new earrings. You are looking at them. I just bought them yesterday at the street market."* And then continue on with the caregiving activity. If the adult is in a hurry to get a task done, she will miss the bonding opportunities that arise from the pleasure of being together.

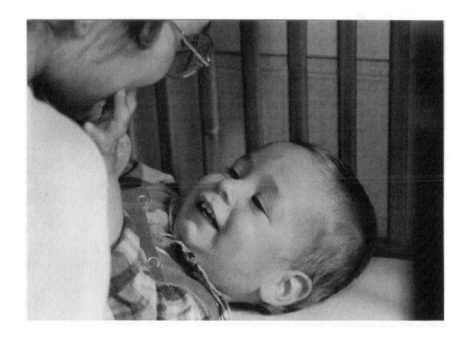

A moment of togetherness at the Pikler residential nursery. Photo from the archives of the Pikler Institute.

Because the first experiences are crucial for the child developing his personality, he needs to feel that he is being addressed, that the person in front of him is truly engaged and awaiting his response to her voice and gestures. He will learn to relax his body and build trust in the adult caring for him.

Excerpt by Dr. Mária Vincze:[29]

"Why is cooperation so essential? Why can we not be satisfied with caregivers talking to the child kindly and handling them gently? Considerate, kind care is, of course, very important in and of itself. Since the infant is at our mercy, he may easily turn into an "object" in the hands of an insensitive caregiver: an object that can be touched, picked up, laid down, pushed around on the diapering table without attention being paid to his balance; an object that can be insensitively manipulated; an object that does not understand or have a command of language, implying that there is no need to talk to him.

So the pushing around can take place in complete silence or something is talked about over his head as the adults in the room carry on a conversation with each other. However, this "object" can see the face bending over him, can hear the words flying above him, and can feel when he is touched. If he is touched with gentle hands, the care situation will not be an uncomfortable experience for the infant.

However, it is not enough. It is during the care situations in the first few weeks and months of life when the infant acquires his first experiences that will be crucial for the later development of his personality; the kind words and gentle care are not enough. He needs to feel that the friendly words are really addressed to him, that the person bending over him really expects an answer with her eyes, her words, and her hands seeking his glance, attention, smile, and his voice responding to her voice.

---

29 Vincze, Maria. *BUPCITI.* pp. 39–41.

He needs to feel that the hands touching his body are asking hands; and he can answer the question by relaxing, loosening his muscles and dissolving his tension. Or on the contrary, he will respond by increasing his tension, his resistance.

That way, the infant can experience that his signals are being recognized and understood, that his needs are taken seriously, and that he is able to respond effectively. In other words, he experiences, from the very beginning, the sensation of being competent and can gradually recognize his "self" and his needs. This way, he can begin to establish a trust that substantiates his personality.

This kind of dialogue between the adult and the child, however, can only emerge if the child is accustomed to really being paid attention to during care and the words are really addressed to him. Cooperation can only develop in an atmosphere characterized by permanently responding to each other."

Voice of Experience: Barbara Rios-Brenes[30]

Zuly, one of the resident patients at our Pediatric Cancer Lodge in Puerto Rico, was excited that day. She chose a beautiful dress with pink and yellow flowers. The big bow on her head didn't compare to her bright smile. Her love poured out, and one couldn't help but feel captivated by the sweet little princess. For Zuly, the feeling of comfortable and clean clothes was great; she loved her pajamas, but today was a special day. Her loving nurse came into her room and played with her.

Noticing the floral patterns on her dress, Mimi made sure to compliment how beautiful Zuly looked. She picked her up and held her with her warm arms. Soon after, she showed the happy hand, a glove filled with air and featuring a big smile drawn with a red pen.

Zuly knew that soon they would remove the needle from her port. This process was scary for her because sometimes it hurt. But Zuly was curious about the process, and the nurse let her touch some of the materials she used to complete the needle removal.

---

30 Barbara Rios-Brenes is director of Children's Hope Lodge of the American Cancer Society in Puerto Rico. See CONTRIBUTORS page for her biography.

She was not afraid and trusted Mimi to do it gently. She was ready to have the needle removed from her chest. She was no longer attached to the medical equipment. This was such a good feeling for her. She could now move her body freely and enjoy all the games on her first birthday party at the oncology hospital.

Zuly never had the chance to celebrate another birthday, but the image of her beautiful smile and happy giggles will live as a vivid memory for the hospital staff and me. We were able to offer her moments of joy and connection.

Life is so short, especially when a small child experiences great health challenges. That's why we need to love, support, and develop a positive relationship with the children we care for. Their emotional needs must become our emotional needs. If we can do this, even the worst health challenges cannot break a child.

Zuly, a fighter and happy child, was a strong baby who spent most of her short life at the hospital. But each time I saw her, she shared her hope through her incredible smile, with the nurses and doctors becoming her loving family. Some days she felt really weak because of the chemotherapy, but she knew that her caregiver was there for her, making her feel safe and soothed.

But all children have the right to feel loved, supported, and close to one adult that cares for their physical and emotional development, with the caregiver paying close attention to understanding how the child is feeling during each interaction. Adults may often ignore the feelings and the emotional well-being of the child, which, to me, is unacceptable, as the respect for the child as an individual must never be taken as unimportant.

Chapter 2.3

The Right to Individuality

All children have the right to be treated as individuals so that their physical and psychological needs are met; they are not hurried, and they end up being satisfied as well as have their own personal belongings.[31]

Observation

The key to our responsiveness is how well we observe. It is through careful observation of each child that a caregiver can come to know his needs and offer individualized attention. Because observation can be cold, we are speaking about seeing the child as a unique person, getting acquainted with him, being interested in him, paying close attention to interpret what he feels and what he knows. It is through being interested and curious that one can truly come to know each child distinctly.

The success of the children's upbringing in an institution depends on the adults taking care of them and on how well they carry out their tasks. It is important that caregivers provide emotional stability. This means that the caregivers must, at all times, be aware of their own emotional stability and focus on the children's needs separate from their own.

By observing the development of children under their care with interest, curiosity, and pleasure, they can provide security as they create the foundation for a stable relationship.

Calling the Child by His First Name

Because it takes time to live a life, one must first create an identity and develop a deeper understanding of oneself. One's name then becomes a factor in developing a sense of self. For this reason, we find it paramount to address each child by his first name.

---

31   Right to personal history added by Dr. Oleg Palmov.

If more than one child in the group has the same first name, we recommend using both first and last name (or first name and first initial of the last name). A name becomes an integral part of each child's individuality. Using nicknames, such as shortening the name Alexander to Alex, or well-intentioned monikers like, *honey, cuddle bear, or sweet pea*, do not in any way help a child develop his self-awareness.

It is recommended that all caregivers in contact with the same child address him in the same manner, avoiding mock names at any cost. In different cultures, children are occasionally nicknamed for the color of their skin or their weight, *Gordito, Flaca, Morenita,* and although these words may be spoken tenderly and with a gentle tone of voice, the impact is profound.

Although the child may not fully understand the meaning, he can intuit that something is wrong with him and, eventually, when he is older, even begin to mock himself in efforts to conceal that he is actually offended by this name. (Kálló, 1995)

A child's given name helps him differentiate himself from the others in his group. When the caregiver says, *"It is Carlyn's turn for her bath,"* the whole group can prepare for what is going to happen. The caregiver may also say, *"Yes, Joanne, I see you. You will have your bath after Zan."*

These verbal cues that incorporate the child's name help him distinguish himself from his peers. As time passes, the child will come to acquire more information about himself because the caregiver is able to speak personally about things that pertain only to him, his moods, his past, present, and future. For this, it is important that the child be allowed to keep his name for the rest of his life.

If adopting parents insist on changing the child's name, we recommend that the child hear his new name from his well-known caregiver, allowing him to get acquainted with the new name. If this doesn't happen and change occurs suddenly around the child—a new home and new, unknown people caring for him—it may cause him to separate from his past. This mental shock may result in a shattering of his self-identity or cause harm to his self-awareness. (Kálló, 1995)

Personal Belongings

It is uncommon in institutions for children to have personal property. But in order for the child to learn to respect others' property, he needs to first understand what it feels like to have his own. If everything is common property, he will never learn to respect others' possessions.

For instance, it is important that the child have his own bed. This will become his personal quiet, private place. In addition, we suggest a few items of clothing that he can claim and recognize as his own. These can be, for example, winter overalls, a coat, or a hat. One or two items will suffice.

To this, we add the importance that each child has one or two toys that are his own. Most toys in the play area will belong to the group. There is a special function of the *own toy*, which Winnicott[32] described as the transitional object. His own toy becomes the object that the child can take when he needs comforting. He can take it to his bed for sleeping or soothing.

It can also happen that this object came with him from home and he got from his mother, but it can also be that this is his cotton scarf/blankie (given to him as an infant at the nursery) or an object that the child chooses from the set of toys among the common toys. After careful observation of his preference for this object, he would be permitted to keep this toy as his own.

Our experience shows that children will respect their own toys (car, doll, blankie) if they have a personal individual attachment to one of the caregivers; if they are not attached to an adult, the toy will mean nothing. This way, if they lose it, they won't even look for it. For this reason, it is not enough to say to the child, *"This is yours."* They have to live the experience of connection to the adult that cares for them.

Colleagues at the Pikler Institute recently found archives that describe the process of gifting children with a special object that

---

32 Winnicott, D. (1953). Transitional objects and transitional phenomena, *International Journal of Psychoanalysis*, 34:89–97.

would become their own. These journal entries describe the time they introduced birthday celebrations. Initially, during the first few years at the institute, it was trial and error, and although the children had a personal relationship with the caregiver, they still didn't have a concept of *"what's mine."* Because of this, a choreography was worked out that later became routine.

A few days before a child's birthday, he was told, *"Gregory, you will be getting this particular toy for your birthday,"* and the other children would be told that this particular toy would become Gregory's property. This allowed children to build the anticipation of the particular object.

A child at the Pikler Institute opening his birthday present. Photo by Marian Reismann from the Pikler archives.

Gregory would be looking forward to his present, and his peers will respect that this would become his own. Gregory would have the privilege of sharing his toy if he wanted to out of his own volition, but he would never be forced to share his own toy if he didn't want to.

On his third birthday, Gregory was invited on an excursion to a store in the city, where he would then pick out his own present. This gave him the opportunity to assert his personal preference and support the building of his self-esteem: He had a voice, and he was respected for expressing it.

Birthday celebrations were memorable. The tradition was for children to wear special clothes that were different from their daily clothes. Different food would also be prepared, and all the other children would get a small gift as well. The concept was of a shared celebration and to share one another's joy.

Caregiver lighting candles during a birthday celebration at the Pikler Institute. Photo by Marian Reismann from the Pikler archives.

Sharing joy during a birthday celebration at the Pikler Institute. Photo by Marian Reismann from the Pikler archives.

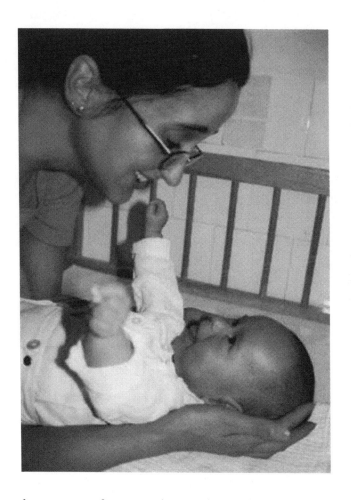

A shared moment of connection and togetherness at the Pikler residential nursery. Photo from the archives of the Pikler Institute.

The Joy of Caregiving

The joyful time together lets the child know that he is accepted and loved as an individual.

Caregiving can become a pleasurable experience for both the adult and the child, instead of often being recognized as a laborious task. Respectful care can have a ripple effect, and it starts with self-awareness. By consciously addressing each child individually in an attentive, caring manner, the child will internalize this type of care, and his own interactions with others will be positively affected.

"One has only to ask and the child will cooperate," said Dr. Pikler.

Taking into account this premise, there is a willing disposition and shift in attitude. By being present with one child at a time and eliciting his cooperation, both adult and child are mutually fueled and left replenished for interaction with the next child that may need one-on-one attention.

The caregiver exhibits joy during caregiving, and the child, in turn, feels that his individuality is respected.

The Role of Language in Caregiving

What Speech Adds to the Caregiver-Child Relationship

When interacting with young children, our voices and tones also play a key role. Just like the gesture of our hands and moving at a slow rhythm, our goal is to invite collaboration and make the interaction pleasurable and enjoyable for all involved.

The child can perceive when the adult is being mechanical during the caregiving routines and wanting to get things done quickly. Instead of this important time together becoming an opportunity for connection, it then becomes a dreaded time for both.

A caregiver needs to be interested in the child, as well as in the child's own interests. She needs to provide a shared history, invite a child's participation, and foster his connection with each other. During the caregiving routines, it is important that she gives information about what is happening: describe the situation in detail and offer suggestions.

By presenting choices and acknowledging his positive behavior, the caregiver will impart a sense of belonging to the child. This, in turn, facilitates transitions, allowing the child to have a positive self-image.

Chapter 2.4

The Right to Protection and Freedom from Aggression

All children have the right to be protected from all types of aggression, open or hidden, verbal, emotional or physical, and have the right to experience the acceptance and respect every human being is entitled to.

Aggression is abuse. No human being should ever be a subject of mistreatment or force. There are different levels of aggression, and we speak here about mini-aggression when the adult doesn't realize he is being violent.

A baby or young child should never be treated with anything other than absolute reverence. In a group situation, aggression on the part of the adult can spread easily because of mechanical treatment of the children. The more impersonal the relationship, the easier it will be for the adult to become aggressive, especially when a child is crying or has behavioral issues.

Acting violently toward children doesn't necessarily have to do with physical or verbal force but could also be the result of not accepting the child or expecting him to be anything other than he is.

In his book, *The Silence of the Sea*, Jean Bruller Vercors makes reference to the hands and how easily they can turn violent without our mindful awareness and how gestures don't lie.

"I learned that day that, to anyone who knows how to observe them, the hands can betray emotions as clearly as the face—as well as the face and better—for they are so subject to the control of the will . . . And the fingers of that hand were stretching and bending, were squeezing and clutching, were abandoning themselves to the most violent mimicry, while his face and his body remained controlled and motionless."[33]

---

33 Jean Bruller [Vercors], *The Silence of the Sea*. Bloomsbury Academic, 2014. p. 91.

When faced with a challenge, the adult must work very diligently to overcome her own reactivity and remain centered at all times when relating with children. The adult becoming aware of her touch, making it personable and gentle, will not subject the child to the harshness during his handling.

Because children will test us, will cry to catch our attention, and will take a little longer to accomplish a task than what we had scheduled according to our own expectations, this is no reason for us to become aggressive toward them. An adult must work with continuous patience and presence to maintain equanimity and emotional balance.

That said, all aggression is damaging and traumatic. Aside from the obvious aggression that may be considered abusive (hitting, spanking, scolding, punitive ignorance, shame, embarrassment), violence can also be subtler and can often be ignored and disregarded if one is not paying close attention to the importance of gentle care.

A baby that is not considered a participant in his care and is simply at the whim of the adult's agenda could very well be experiencing a form of violence. For example: when after a bath, an adult unexpectedly swoops an infant from a supine to a prone position with rushed movements and without telling him in advance what is going to happen or when a sitting child is quickly put on a supine position instead of being asked to lie down on his own.

This would not only be shocking, but also, he may perhaps even bang his head falling backward. When the child is able to sit on his own, he can already be asked to finish the movement.

Thus, not only do we prevent him from lying down by himself, but we are also adding to the situation the disagreeable experience of a sudden loss of balance, which could result in a hard landing on the changing surface. From that, the child does not learn that togetherness with his caretaker offers the opportunity for cooperation, and the mood for playful dialogue will not be stirred in him.

Fostering Nonviolence

How can an infant or young child experience his own competence if his caregiver's hands are rude and in a hurry to finish a task?

As we have mentioned before, the hands of the adult need to be quiet and patient. Her open hands symbolize the gestures of offering and receiving. This expression invites the child to a possibility of choices and is able to meet the caregiver halfway.

There's a thought process that is happening in the child. *"She offers, I receive. She waits receptively, I give of myself."* There is a mutually respectful dialogue between the two. The hands also pose a question: *"Are you ready for me?"*

Because the hands are asking, this nonviolent way of being together offers the child an opportunity to assert his free will. The adult is encouraged to wait for an answer, the relationship is being enriched, and there is harmony in this way of being together.

We encourage the adult to not grab anything out of the child's hand with force. By modeling this behavior, the child is learning to, in turn, be kind with the adults and his peers. We don't need to teach him to be kind because he is internalizing the appropriate way of interacting with another from his own experiences during his care.

There is an anecdote about a few children playing at a swimming pool in Budapest in the 1940s. They were near the pool playing with balls when the attendant told the children that they were not allowed to play with balls there. It was hard, however, for the children to stop, and the attendant said, *"If you don't stop, I will slap you."*

Assertively, one child responded, *"You cannot hit me, I am a Pikler child."* This child was Agnes Szanto-Feder.[34] An excerpt from one of her articles is included in Right 6, *The Right To Activity.*

The Importance of Gentle Tactile Communication by Anna Tardos

Being touched is, if only through the motions of regular caregiving, part of daily life for the baby. Through the manner in which he is being touched, important messages of intimacy, love, and

---

34   See CONTRIBUTORS page for Dr. Agnes Szanto-Feder's biography.

awareness are being conveyed to him, which are sometimes better understood than words alone.

An infant, and also a young child, must rely on adult protection and help and, thus, is extremely dependent upon her and very sensitive to the way he is touched. Let us imagine how big the adult caretaking hands are in relation to the infant's body. Let us imagine that someone, whose hands are the size of a baby's entire back, would take care of us.

Touch is not necessarily loving and full of respect, but it can be disagreeable and even menacing. Adults similarly experience that careless and aggressive closeness and touch can be uncomfortable and are able to recoil from it.

Why is it important to mention this here? The adult carries the infant, takes care of him, and during all this, touches him with her hands. Often in that circumstance, the adult fails to be aware of how she touches him and, thus, doesn't notice when her movements cause him disagreeable sensations.

It can, therefore, happen that the infant experiences both friendly care and a disagreeable touch. Those antagonistic messages can confuse him, making him insecure and distrustful. The infant and the young child express their feelings about how the adult touches them or handles their bodies. If he enjoys the touch, even the newborn will curl up in the hands that encompass him.

When the infant's care is agreeable to him, he will feel good during changing, bathing, dressing, and undressing and will gradually relax. In a way, he prepares himself to be picked up. He relaxes in advance the limbs that are next in line for washing or clothing and cooperatively continues the movement that the adult has begun.

If the experience of the adult's hands is frequently linked to disagreeable sensations, however, the child may look forward to the end of the undressing-changing-dressing procedure with resistance. Oftentimes the newborn will twitch when the adult's hand touches him suddenly and without warning.

I will describe in the following a number of frequent and repetitive movements with which adults unintentionally cause the child disagreeable and sometimes painful situations. These examples may foster increased awareness of the effects of careless handling.

The general well-being of the young child depends in large part upon the way he is being touched by the adult. The experience with children living in homes remains unsettling in that regard.

When the adult wants to change the natural, spontaneous position of the child's head, his arms, or his legs in order to clean the body wrinkles, for example, and doesn't wait for the child to be prepared to let her have his limbs by relaxing his muscles, she will only achieve her goal by winning over that very resistance. To this end, she will often require a use of force. This is how the adult's movements become hard and violent for the child.

Another occasion of discomfort for the infant is the constant disturbance of his balance. As a consequence of lack of head support when being picked up, the infant often tries desperately to avoid the uncoordinated movements of his head.

Wrongly acquired movements of the adult that have become routine may be another source of unpleasant experience for the infant. A caregiver has to pick up a number of infants daily, for instance, lie them down on the changing table, change them, feed them, and lie them back down in their beds or wherever they've been playing. The constant repetition of these situations and actions can have a negative reflection on the quality of her movements.

Movements that are repeated as part of a work routine usually become shorter, faster, and slightly mechanical. This is known to be the case, for example, with proficient shorthand typists, lab technicians, or weavers who perform part of their work successfully with deft movements, without having to pay attention to details.

If, however, the movements directly related to the handling of the child are performed rapidly and mechanically, if she is treating the child as she does an object, then there is serious danger.

Swift and mechanical movements do not allow the child to get ready for what is happening to him and to actively participate in it. In fact, they actually exclude him. Some routine movements aim at preventing the participation of the child in order to speed up the care.

These movements generally contain violent elements and prevent the possibility of the infant and the toddler enjoying the care process. In addition, these specific and swift movements completely exclude other forms of interaction between the child and his caregiver, i.e., eye contact.

The way the adult handles the child conveys a number of messages to him. Quick, harsh movements are transmitters of inattentiveness, impatience, and sometimes also indifference and do not express compassion. These experiences tend to obstruct the creation of relationship.

The adult sometimes brings the child from a sitting position to a lying position, completely unexpectedly, without telling the child in advance what is going to happen to him or asking him to lie down. This may cause the child to tilt abruptly on his back. Thus, not only do we prevent him from lying down by himself, but we also add the disagreeable experience of a sudden loss of balance, as well as a hard landing on the changing table.

The same goes for movements wherein a prone infant is suddenly pulled up by his arms into a sitting or standing position. This transmits the message to the child that whatever is happening to him and with him is not worth noticing, is not an important event, and that he himself is not valued as a person.

As a result, the child does not learn that togetherness with his caregiver can be pleasant; neither does he learn that this togetherness offers the opportunity of cooperation.

When the adult takes a child that is already walking by the wrist and pulls him in a certain direction or pushes his head or his back, she is sending a negative message to the child. Her actions neither allow for nor support his independence. She is also not trusting that the child will come when called to come.

In this particular way of leading a child, no attention whatsoever is paid to the child's own rhythm.

These may be somewhat harsh examples, but they are commonplace and readily observed. This is not to say, however, that interest in more respectful handling of children is not growing in institutions.

Our experience of several decades at Lóczy illustrate that the mechanical and routine-like handling of children can be prevented. In the course of our work with other institutions and day-care employees, we saw that the adult can free herself from the quick and mechanical, unkind, and oppressing movements that have been learned through inadequate caregiving.

When someone manages to become aware of a child's reactions to her own hands, these hands will more readily touch the infant in a respectful manner. I want to mention a few principles that we follow at Lóczy.

When carrying or holding the infant in one's arms, it is important to support his whole trunk and head in order for him not to lose the feeling of physical safety.

Harmonious experiences during togetherness in care situations enrich the relationship of the adult taking care of the child. Her hands are a source of important experiences for the infant and the small child.

The adult's movements during the handling of the child do not only influence his bodily experiences, but her gentle and caring gestures convey attentiveness and interest as well.

It is sometimes easier to first speak to the child kindly and then follow an action with careful hands. I want to draw attention to our own hands in order for us to increasingly make conscious use of our hands and what we convey to the infant and toddler through them.

Voice of Experience: Dr. Natasha Khazanov[35]

As the African American social reformer, orator, and statesman Frederick Douglass once said, "It is easier to build strong children than to repair broken adults." Indeed, in looking at the first three years of a child's life, one can see how those years shape the infant's

---

35 Natasha Khazanov, Ph.D., is a neuropsychologist and psychotherapist. See CONTRIBUTORS page for her biography.

future, his connection to the world, and his personal relationships. Yes, a child is born with a defined temperament, but his personality will be shaped through his interactions with the environment. How each child is able to build resilience depends on the fortune of having an attachment figure that can help him or her overcome a difficult beginning.

As an associate clinical professor at UCSF School of Medicine, I teach both students and residents. Having also assessed more than 80 criminals convicted of committing brutal murders, as well as having served as an expert witness in criminal cases, I found all these individuals to have had a history of early trauma created by adverse childhood experiences.

Because of these findings, what I call a tragedy generations in the making, I came to understand the role of trauma caused by parental abuse, neglect, and abandonment and how these traumas then affect the developing brain and the mind.

When our EI (emotional intelligence) is not in keeping with our IQ (intelligence quotient), society pays a huge price. We are wired to be good, empathic, and compassionate, but deviating from this path generally results in trauma. Our society is dealing with consequences of the violence that happens when we are not cared for.

I recently developed the SMARTT program, an acronym of the words safety, mindfulness, attunement, resilience, trust, *and* tenacity. *SMARTT is a kind of "brain checklist."*[36]

SMARTT helps guide adults to parent from the "inside out" by modeling emotional intelligence and self-compassion. My mix of evidence-based, neuroscience-informed approaches focuses not only on the relationship between adult and child, but also on the relationship to self.

I truly believe that good parents can change the world, to which I can also add, and good caregivers can change the world as well.

---

36 *SMARTT parenting is designed to help loving and attuned parents avoid making parenting mistakes by incorporating evidence-based techniques.* http://smarttparenting.com.

Child development specialists have published decades of research supporting the premise that the environment of a child's earliest years creates profound effects, including building the foundation of resilience and the ability to bounce back. Conversely, if things go wrong during this crucial period when the child's brain is developing, he will experience a heightened susceptibility to mental and physical illness, among other negative effects of early trauma.

The first three years of life are thought to be an especially critical period because it is during these years that the synaptic density in the area of the brain that is referred to as the organ of civilization (prefrontal cortex) increases dramatically. (Synaptic density refers to the density of neurons in the brain, and it is this density that will indicate how this area functions. In essence, the denser the area, the better the functioning of the brain.)

Making use of the SMARTT program helps mitigate the negative effects on a child who is placed in a residential care facility and allows that child the opportunity to enjoy a healthy and happy life.

My lifelong fascination with the brain and the mind began when I was an undergraduate psychology student at Leningrad State University in 1974 and attended Dr. Alexander Luria's lecture about the frontal lobes. Dr. Luria was a brilliant Russian neurologist and neuropsychologist whose research in the brain was revolutionary and ahead of his time.

In more than 30 years of clinical practice, I came across many stories relating to trauma, posttraumatic vulnerabilities, and posttraumatic growth. During these decades, new brain-imaging technologies have opened the doors to create a better understanding of what Dr. Luria and Dr. Pikler established using their clinical knowledge and intuition in the post-WWII era.

Equipped with the evidence provided by the booming field of neuroscience, we can substantiate scientific evidence that supports Dr. Pikler's effective approach for rearing children in residential care facilities.

There are two important discoveries in helping understand this:

1. *Our brains are capable of changing in response to our experiences and, in fact, are continually rewiring themselves. This phenomenon can be captured in the notion of neuroplasticity, the term that describes lasting change to the brain throughout an individual's life.*
2. *Safe, supportive, and warm relationships help promote our brain's positive neuroplasticity, which has been pioneered by Dr. Daniel Siegel in the field of interpersonal neurobiology.*

Furthermore, Siegel has said that we can foster secure attachments if we remember the four Ss:

- *Seen - This is not just seeing with the eyes but means perceiving children deeply and empathically, as well as sensing the mind behind their behavior.*
- *Safe - We avoid actions and responses that frighten or hurt children.*
- *Soothed - We help them deal with difficult emotions and situations.*
- *Secure - We help them develop an internalized sense of well-being.*

Thus, when the baby feels seen, safe, secure, and soothed in the presence of a caregiver, the four Ss help promote brain integration and growth. This feeling of safety in the body also negates the need for dissociation and promotes neurogenesis (neural growth) in the areas of the brain that are of crucial importance for cognitive and emotional development.[37]

As an expert in the neurobiology of trauma, I understand that early experiences that overwhelm children can also create emotional disregulation and may lead to a lifelong struggle.

---

37 Daniel J. Siegel, MD; Tina Payne Bryson, PhD. 2012. *Whole Brain Child*. Bantam Books.

One of the landmark studies that proved this is the Adverse Childhood Experiences (ACE) study. Published by Kaiser Permanente and Center for Disease Control in the late '90s, the ACE study established that exposure to early adversity affects the brain development and is linked to poor physical and mental health, as well as premature death in those who had higher number of ACEs.

"Childhood experiences, both positive and negative, have a tremendous impact on future violence, victimization and perpetration, and lifelong health and opportunity. As such, early experiences are an important public health issue." Much of the foundational research in this area has been referred to as Adverse Childhood Experiences (ACEs).[38]

Parental separation also contributes to an adverse experience that is often compounded by other traumatic experiences, such as physical and emotional abuse and neglect, sexual abuse, parental mental illness, and domestic violence. It is now understood that these experiences affect development of those areas of the brain that are involved in emotional regulation, impulse control, learning, executive functioning, and the pleasure and reward center of the brain.

This has been implicated in substance abuse, where the pleasure and reward system of the brain that may have been affected by childhood experiences, will likely lead to the adult becoming addicted to substances.

High number of ACEs also affect a developing immune system, endocrine system, and even one's DNA. Children who enter residential care facilities often have several ACEs, which, at times, result in behavioral and medical problems.

The mechanism of these negative effects of early trauma lies within our brain's ability to help us survive by creating the state of dissociation or the "numbing" effect and, thus, easing the pain of a repeated adverse experience.

---

38   http://nationalcac.org/professionals/images/M_images/ace%20study%20 overview.pdf.

The most traumatic levels of dissociation occur in babies exposed to traumatic experiences preverbally, creating the state of chronic heightened alertness and agitation and inhibiting the development of the important areas of the brain involved in functions associated with emotional intelligence, as well as cognitive and social functioning.

The antidote to the lasting negative effects of trauma lies within the human connection. For babies who live in children's homes, it lies in the hands of their caregivers.

Looking at the protective factors that mitigate the lasting negative effects of early stressful experiences, the importance of positive attachments must be emphasized. Since our brain is being shaped by the world around us, there is hardly a more effective intervention than creating a safe connection with the child, especially one that may not have felt safe for a long period.

It has also been shown that a safe, gentle touch lowers stress hormones and promotes a sense of safety and security, ultimately changing the brain's wiring and function. Babies may not know the words yet, but we communicate with them constantly. We can communicate "You are not safe with me" by being rushed, distracted, or intrusive.

Conversely, safety is telegraphed by our "attuned presence" or what Dr. Siegel cites, along with presence and resonance, as the way we clinically create the essential condition of trust. Safe touch, quality of voice, and facial expressions are also desired elements that give babies the feeling of being safe.

That is the core premise of Dr. Pikler's approach, or what Stephen Porges calls the neuroception of safety, which is the idea that the baby's endocrine system stops secreting stress hormones and produces instead neurotransmitters that promote healthy brain development and healing.

Finally, I believe Dr. Pikler's approach is the system that, when implemented in residential care facilitates, will have a huge positive impact on the developing brain and create the mind that is geared to a life of success. In other words, I suggest that effective caregivers can—and do—change the world.

That is the relationship that heals.

Chapter 2.5

The Right to Continuity and Predictability

All children have the right to continuity and stability in their personal relationships, physical environment, and life circumstances, including a predictable organization of events in their everyday lives.

Personal Relationships

To support children in their development of self-esteem, there must be a stable, real, and personal relationship between children and the adults that care for them. This connection will bring children positive effects that will carry on throughout their entire lives.

Personal relationships become personal by having the same caregivers continuously caring for the same child. This stability gives way to a healthy attachment only if the child and caregiver can really come to know each other. It is difficult for the relationship to be personal if there is always a different caregiver, a stranger, or volunteers that rotate regularly. Three or four alternating adults are fine, but it would not be beneficial for the child to have, for instance, 25 different people involved in his daily care, which is the case sometimes.

This is probably the most difficult part of the implementation and why we recommend creating a schedule where all adults working at a children's home follow a uniformed consistency. This means that the same adults are working with the same groups of children and are also carrying out their tasks in a similar way. In addition, the order in which the children are cared for is to be honored. (During feeding, for example, Jenny will go after Ralph and Lupe after Gonzalo).

For children in institutions, particularly, consistency gives them a renewed sense of order that allows them to develop trust and feel secure. Thanks to the element of predictability, they can count on their needs being met and feel joy in the relationship.

Indeed, the caregivers at the Pikler Institute were instructed to hold the infants in a similar manner, with the same choreographed movements. These women remain peaceful when interacting with each child in a similar, consistent way because they have had thorough training, a vital part of the Pikler program.

If possible, it is a good idea for caregivers to first practice this particular way of holding and speaking with a baby by using baby dolls, as seen in this picture during a training session at the Pikler Institute.

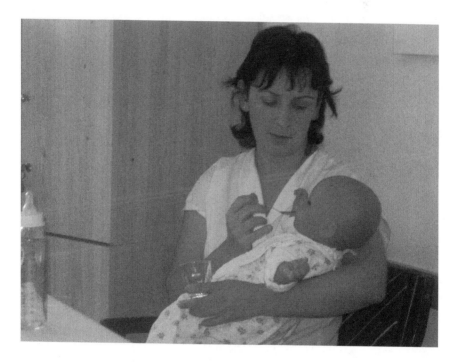

Group leader Jutka Kelemen demonstrates how to hold an infant during a feeding at Pikler Institute. Photo by Elsa Chahin.

Each baby, therefore, would become comfortable in a certain way of being held and anticipate what will come next, no matter if the morning caregiver was different from the afternoon or evening one. Within the particular way of holding the child, the adult has her own freedom to interact in a natural fashion, uniquely adapting to each child's innate rhythm. She is encouraged to bathe the child with language as she weaves in past, present, and future events in the child's life.

By saying *"This morning you had bananas. In the afternoon, you will have applesauce with your meal,"* the caregiver reassures the child that she is familiar with important details in the child's life.

"In the afternoon, when you wake up, Kati is going to take care of you" lets the child know that the caregiver is present in the events about to occur in the child's life. Her soft voice is soothing and reassures the child that she is present for him.

This also helps give the caregiver a more profound purpose during their interactions: They learn to become involved and make the relationship personal.

It is not about independence but interdependence and the adult being present for that child. For example, the caregiver allows the older child to put on his shoe on his own, but she doesn't leave him alone to do it. She assists him, and if the child cannot do it, she finishes the task.

Indeed, all the children living at the Pikler Institute were cared for with respect, and they felt part of a group. In fact, they were learning to wait their turn! They saw that the caregiver fed and took care of other children too, meaning that they knew when their turn would come. They were sure that, when this moment came, they would be the center of their caregiver's attention.

Voice of Experience: Diane Harkins, PhD[39]

First and foremost, continuity means that children have access to consistent, caring adults who support them in the daily routines of living—eating, bathing, diapering, and toileting. Ideally, these children and their adult caregivers are in small groups. Whenever possible, they continue together as a group as the children grow and develop.

---

39 Diane Harkins, PhD, is an early childhood specialist at WestEd. See CONTRIBUTORS page for her biography.

Continuity is considered to be one aspect of quality care. It is a preferred practice in programs that serve children who have families to go home to each evening. Yet this right is often denied to children in residential care. Globally, it is estimated that young children in residential care have contact with dozens of caregivers before the age of five.

For an infant, this means that one person may diaper the child at 8:00 a.m. and another person may diaper him at noon. A different person may feed them, if they are actually held and fed by an adult. As days and months go by, these children miss the opportunity to form a relationship with consistent, responsive adults, a necessary ingredient for healthy attachments and social-emotional development.

Residential programs that have adopted aspects of the Pikler approach are not only characterized by consistent adults and small groups, but also that the emotional climate of the setting is warm. Adults are calm and unhurried, encouraging each child's participation in the routines as they look for ways to increase their engagement with the task at hand.

As an example, I remember an observation I made in a residential facility that had received training in responsive caregiving, one where I was in the process of creating greater consistency for the children.

A staff person was feeding breakfast to a toddler with special needs. The woman and child sat facing each other, both in child-size chairs. The caregiver spoon-fed the child his breakfast, waiting while he chewed and swallowed his food before offering him another spoonful.

She spoke to him about the taste and texture of the food, at the same time making eye contact with him. These may seem like simple practices that could be adopted by any caregiver in any residential facility, yet there are significant challenges to creating a warm, responsive atmosphere.

One of the greatest challenges to continuity is the development of a staffing schedule that meets the needs of the children while also ensuring that adult work schedules are manageable, realistic, and consistent with local labor laws.

Considerations include poor public transportation, staff responsibilities to their own families, and inadequate budgets, to name a few. Yet continuity can be achieved, reducing the number of caregivers to a maximum of four or five people who interact with a group of children on a daily or weekly basis.

Coupled with training in responsive care, this change in the infrastructure can have a powerful effect on the well-being of both children and adults in residential programs.

Physical Environment

Children living in an institution must feel at home because this is their home for however long they reside in it. For this reason, their living space must be designed in a way that their activities support their ever-growing needs and development.

There is no need for the children to change from room to room. It is beneficial if the child can stay in the same room and the furnishings, the material conditions of play and care, can be adapted according to his growing needs.

Predictability of Regimen

Children not only feel secure when they can predict what will happen, but they also come to anticipate the caregiver's next move and can, thus, cooperate. Caregiving routines done in the same way every time allow the child to develop a sense of security. He knows what will be happening; he has a sense of order in his life.

Dr. Pikler observed that when cared for in the same gentle way and in the same sequence, babies and young children were able to relax their bodies in a matter of days. She also noticed that, after a few weeks, they would be able to shape their mouths when being spoken to during their care. She eventually found that the child would cooperate in a more active way when the caregiving routines were predictable and performed in the same manner.

By the caregiver preparing the environment ahead of time, the child comes to understand the cues of what is to come next. If it is time to eat, for example, the caregiver may prepare the table with tablecloth, plates, and anything else she may need for the feeding. Seeing this preparation alerts the child of what is to come next.

A feeding corner at the Pikler Daycare Center. Photo by Julianne Payne.

Voice of Experience: Ruth Mason[40]

Eighteen-month-old Balasz, who was born prematurely and is blind, is having a bath. He is reclining on his back, bouncing his long thin body up and down, and splashing water everywhere. His caregiver, Jutka, who is supporting his head with her left arm, is leaning away from the bath (which is at waist height), her body concave, the front of her T-shirt and cotton pants soaking wet.

The bathroom floor is flooded, but Jutka pays no attention to all that. Her gaze, her smile, and her focus is solely on Balasz, enveloping him in affection. She talks to him in a relaxed manner,

---

40 Ruth Mason is an Israel-based journalist who has written extensively about parents and children. See CONTRIBUTORS page for her biography.

joining him, as it were, in this activity, as he keeps splashing away, his buttocks moving rhythmically up and down. This goes on for several minutes.

When she takes him gently out of the bath, Jutka tells Balasz what she is doing, even though he is hard of hearing. Jutka wraps him in a soft white towel and places him gently on the changing table adjacent to the bathtub. Before she begins drying him, Jutka leans in closely and talks to Balasz, her voice soothing, gentle. He coos back, his non-seeing eyes fixed solidly on her face, enraptured.

After she dries him, Jutka lays a T-shirt on Balasz's chest and pats it, saying, "I'm putting on your tricot." Putting her hand through a sleeve, she asks for his arm, giving it a little tap, and waits until he lifts it. She lets him feels the diaper before she puts it on him as she explains what she is doing.

Every so often, Jutka leans in closer and talks to Balasz softly, sometimes caressing his head as she speaks. They are involved with each other, clearly enjoying the contact. The flow of love, communication, connection, and respect from Jutka to Balasz swells the heart.

It has taken Jutka a long time to bathe and dress Balasz, and when she is done, she slowly lifts him and cuddles him face-to-face. He reaches out and touches her mouth.

The following is an excerpt from the summary of *BUPCITI* outlining the most important aspects of the work at infants' homes[41]:

> "One of the most painful aspects and a major obstacle of the development of infants and young children separated from their families is the lack of stability that impedes the continuousness of their lives. Stability and continuousness are the underlying factors that substantiate a child's tranquility and emotional security, enabling them to have the motivation to be active and be interested in the world.

---

41   Written by experts at the Pikler Institute, Falk, Hevesi, Kálló, Tardos, Pikler, Vincze. Pp. 156, 157.

But it is also the precondition of being capable of finding out about the world; of orientating amid the relationships of surrounding objects and people, as well as the various phenomena of life; of creating appropriate notions, concepts, and memories; and of acquiring the age-appropriate knowledge. Last but not least, it is also the precondition of creating the appropriate image of themselves and their place in the world.

Hence, the lack of this continuousness of life is a major obstacle of the emotional, cognitive, and social development of infants and young children growing up in an ever-changing environment. Every time the environment, the objects, and the people around the child change, there will be different habits and different foods, as well as different requirements made on him.

The situation of the child within his environment will also change. His new environment will see him differently, and he will also mean something different to his new caregiver and peers from the old ones that he was accustomed to. His past is shattered.

Unless the conditions of stability and continuousness are established deliberately and in a well-designed manner, with the minute details of everyday life organized properly, the children will find no "handholds," they will have difficulties in creating their own self-image, and they will not find their place in their material and personal environment. They will also be unable to embrace other opportunities of daily activities or care situations, which, however, should be the main occasions for individual relationships.

In order to establish the sense of security, guaranteeing continuousness should be the underlying principle of all institutions. The necessity of continuousness ranges over all domains of the children's lives, including the material environment. Rooms and furniture play a key role in ensuring that the children find themselves in a familiar environment at any given time while playing or being cared for and allows them to find the things known to them, including their personal belongings, in their usual places."

Chapter 2.6

The Right to Activity

All children should be able to satisfy their natural need for activity, to have the possibility of moving and playing freely, discovering their surroundings, and developing their capacities.

Still today many believe that in order for a child to learn to crawl, to walk, and to play, he needs to be taught. It is a natural need of infants and young children to be active and be interested in the surrounding world and to move. In the course of these actions, the child is able to learn and develop in his own rhythm.

In an institutional setting, it is especially important that they can spend their awake time actively and not to linger or wait for the adult to entertain them. It is especially important for children to be able to experience how to be active, how to move, how to learn from their own experiences, and how to feel pleasure in learning new things without the adult directing him.

The opportunity to move and play freely reinforces the child's trust in himself, i.e., his self-esteem: *I am interested. I decide what to do. I try something new. I learn from my failures and my successes.* In order for the child to have this opportunity, he needs to have recurring time when he can follow his own interest and a spacious area arranged safely and corresponding with his developmental stage. In order to implement all this, it is not necessary for the adult to teach the child how to move and how to play.

Excerpt by Dr. Judit Falk[42]:

> "A new danger lies in the knowledge gained in recent decades about the extraordinary learning capacity of infants and

---

42   Judit Falk, *THE IMPORTANCE OF PERSON-ORIENTED ADULT-CHILD RELATIONSHIPS AND ITS BASIC CONDITIONS, BUPCITI.* P 22

young children. This danger can be met only by refraining fromconditioning children, refraining from teaching them as early as possible, without respite and with inventiveness, things they would learn better on their own and in areas in which they could reach real mastery on their own.

Learning to do what they are taught in these areas is done only in order to please the adult, without the children really understanding what they are doing. Instead of giving them instruction at an early age, the scientific knowledge of the heretofore unimagined abilities in babies could strengthen our trust in the infants' inherent independent learning capacity.

There can be no doubt as to the importance of certain moments in the social situation during which children learn social behavior as well as the use of various utensils as governed by traditional social usage. However, when children play and move freely in activities responsibly undertaken on their own, they experience opportunities to learn that which cannot be simulated and for which there is no substitute.

When an adult interferes with a child's movement and play, not only is there a disturbance of the autonomy of the situation, but also the adult's own goals are substituted for the child's interests, and this intervention creates an unnatural dependency on the adult. In contrast to this monopolizing, autocratic behavior, an attitude of respect on the part of the adult would create the basis for common respect and trust between the adult and the child.

The unfolding of a child's autonomy demands both the emotional stability of a caring relationship and the opportunity for the child to experience his or her own competence through independent activity."

Freedom of Movement

Freedom of movement not only results in outstanding gross motor development, but also a strong sense of competence within each baby who finds out that he can learn on his own and doesn't need an adult. Emotional security and self-confidence are the result.

When you observe, you can see how lively, curious, and self-sufficient the children are, even as infants. They also get along with one another remarkably well.

Allowing children to move freely in their infancy results in good balance, coordination, and calculated risk-taking. Whether in person or on video, anyone who has seen children at the Pikler Institute is impressed by the ease and confidence with which they move their bodies.

Old black-and-white movies from the Pikler Institute show toddlers ascending and descending steep stone steps with all the confidence in the world. They know how to handle their bodies, they have impressive equilibrium, and their body awareness is far above average. Perhaps most importantly, the institute has an extremely low accident rate.

Children from the Pikler® Institute on their way to their garden, exploring their own way of climbing steps with confidence, with their caregiver close by. Photo by Marian Reismann from the Pikler Archives.

As Ruth Mason wrote in her article for the *Jerusalem Post*, "Giving Babies the Best Start in Life," which was later republished in *Exchange Magazine*, *"Pikler babies in Budapest are recognized by the grace and confidence with which they move—even when they are older. This stems from Pikler's notion of what a baby needs for optimal development: space and time for free, uninterrupted play, supported by sensitive, observant attention during slowed-down daily care routines."*

The approach is based on respect for babies as human beings, as well as our capacity to trust in them to develop as they are meant to without our interference or "help."

Children go through a natural set of developmental milestones, meaning that without any intervention, they will all follow the same path. The freely moving children will also go from the back-lying position to walking without any interference. Emmi Pikler first observed it in families as a pediatrician. Later, in the institute, she managed to observe this process in a scientifically controlled environment. She summarized it in her book *Give Me Time,* which is illustrated in the following chart.

From supine to turning onto belly. Stretching and rolling.				
Developmental progress of creeping on belly to crawling on hands and knees				
Developmental progress of sitting up				
Developmental progress of standing up				
From unsupported standing up to walking				

Illustrations by Klara Pap

Here is another excerpt from the summary of BUPCITI outlining the most important aspects of the work at infants' homes.[43]

"All the elements of the physiological process of motor development are based on the internal inclination and the own initiative of the child. A healthy infant or young child does not need an adult to directly interfere with his motor development, either by teaching, exercising, placing the child in certain positions, encouraging, or demanding.

Such interference is not only unnecessary, but it may be harmful as well.

Infants, who are unable to sit up by themselves but are seated, do not have strong enough spinal columns and back muscles to take such a load, and they will sit stiffly with a bent back. If they tilt or lose balance, they will be unable to help themselves. If they are stood on their feet and led by the arms, they will walk awkwardly and clumsily, and wrong balancing and improper conditioning will become their habit.

If there is no external intervention, each infant will *work out* his own ways of turning, rising, and changing position and place that are the most appropriate for the given individual.

The "help" and "teaching" received externally will deprive him of studying the details of each movement to be done. It also deprives the baby of the pleasures of individual initiatives, attempts, and achievements. And as the child will only be able to regain or leave the new positions or do new ones with external help, he will permanently need and, thus, require the constant help of an adult.

However, not interfering in the process of development does not mean that we have no tasks in connection with creating the conditions necessary for the development. It is the task of the adult to provide everything that the children need for their good moods and well-being, their sense of security, and their development.

---

43   Written by experts at the Pikler Institute, Falk, Hevesi, Kálló, Tardos, Pikler, Vincze. p. 175.

Infants will feel like moving around and feel good in their environment only if they can count on their signals getting noticed and responded to, on their needs being fulfilled, and on having enough space and other material conditions available for free movement."

Safety

Already before learning to walk, the child needs to spend his awake time in a spacious playing area where he can roll, creep, crawl, and climb before he comes to the vertical position.

It is important that the play area is 100% safe. This means that the environmental surroundings, as well as the play objects, are equally safe and free of any danger or harm.

Outlets, cords, and shelves that are not attached to the wall pose a huge threat. A young child's innate need for discovery leads him to mouth objects he comes into contact with. Small objects, such as paper clips, marbles, thumbtacks, needles, and anything that fits inside a toilet paper tube, should be avoided, as should cleaning products, medicines, and sharp objects, as they present a choking hazard, poisonous ingestion, or worse.

After careful exploration of the environment, the best device is adult supervision within the safe space. To this we add the notion that the child should have confidence in playing and moving freely, as it is extremely important that he first feels secure in his relationship with his/her caregiver. Once this foundation is secure, the child can branch out to explore and initiate his play.

If there are several children in the play area, the space must be at least one square meter per child, beginning when the child is able to turn from his back onto his side.

A safe area with adequate space allows babies to move freely at the Pikler Institute. Photo by Marian Reismann from the Pikler archives.

Play

Maria Montessori described play as "the child's work" (Montessori, 1967), and biologist Karl Groos (Groos, 1901) wrote about play being a "preparation for life."

A child's life consists, in great part, of play; it is a fundamental need. We feel that every child should be allowed to play, whenever not involved in a caregiving activity. To this we add the concept of free play, not directed or instructed play, but free play where a child can have the opportunity to discover and let his imagination wander.

Dr. Peter Gray, author of *Free to LEARN* (2013), says, *"The decline of free play and the careerist approach to childhood have exacted a heavy toll."*

It is our recommendation to allow each child to fully experience self-initiated activities that he or she enjoys and be allowed to play uninterruptedly, with care providers available should the child need them. It is important to note that children are never made to feel abandoned. If a caregiver in a particular moment is not able to tend to one child because she is bathing, feeding, or diapering another, she will assure the child with her gentle tone of voice that she hears him and will be with him as soon as she is finished.

It may be at times difficult for the adult in the group to resist the temptation of telling the children *how* to play. She may feel that she is not *doing* anything by just being present in the play space among the children. However, one can experience joy when observing play, as it is a different level in the human condition: It is the ability to respect others' needs and desires and not to try to control them at all times.

Freedom of movement also facilitates the development of fine motor skills. At the Pikler Institute, babies have been closely observed. As a result, a great deal of thought has gone into the simple play materials they are offered, playthings that respond to precisely what the children need at each stage of development. The objects need to be arranged in ways that are accessible to children, within reach, and easy to grasp.

Toys and play equipment at the Pikler Daycare Center stimulate both gross motor and manipulation activities. Photo by Julianne Payne.

Because babies are on their backs during their first months of life, they have full use of their hands and arms and can freely explore all that they encounter. The first play materials are simple cotton scarves that babies can pick up, hold, wave, and manipulate. The cotton scarves are introduced at approximately three months of age; before this age, their own hands captivate their curiosity and represent their first experience of discovery.

Instead of toys dangling over children's faces or mobiles hanging above them, children need a variety of appropriate objects that they can grasp, hold, turn, mouth, bang, and drop. Merely looking at brightly colored objects and trying to bat them is a limited, unvaried experience. It is far more interesting to manipulate an object—turning it to see all sides. This is how children learn its various properties.

A child who comes from a difficult situation can find calmness in an object that is predictable. As the child plays, he is able to believe in the consistency of the objects, when he learns that a cube is always a cube. According to Dr. Gabriella Püspöky, resident pediatrician at the Pikler Institute since 1960, children can get through a crisis if they have someone to hold on to, as well as objects and self-initiated activities that interest them.

Self-initiated is a key word used at the Pikler Institute. Adults don't entertain or stimulate children. The babies learn to entertain and stimulate themselves by exploring what their bodies can do, by exploring other babies around them, and by exploring objects and the environment itself. This is quite different from the usual group care situation where someone decides a fussy baby is bored and takes on the job of providing a little entertainment or stimulation, either with a toy or with some kind of activity.

The babies at the Pikler Institute have plenty of activities, and most invent their own with materials available to them.

How children play and explore the environment, with curiosity and engagement, will give caregivers direct feedback about their work. When children are enjoying their play, in a healthy emotional state, it shows that caregivers are connecting with the children during the care routines, and the children feel emotionally fueled and confident to branch out and play independently.

If a child is not in a well-balanced emotional state, he will not engage in independent play, and caregivers can offer to support him through this difficulty, during the care situation, and not by instructing him how to play.

The following is another excerpt from the summary of *BUPCITI*, outlining the most important aspects of the work at infants' homes.[44]

"Since the beginning of time, play has been a natural way of life and a major source of pleasure for young children. Adults need to first provide the conditions where play will unfold, the most important being the following:

---

44 Written by experts at the Pikler Institute, Falk, Hevesi, Kálló, Tardos, Pikler, Vincze. pp. 177–180.

- Protection and tranquility. Children who feel safe and whose basic needs have been satisfied can play enthusiastically and with pleasure.
- Possibility of movement. Movement is a basic need for children, and free movement requires plenty of space.
- Time. Children need the possibility to play freely without getting interrupted.
- Toys. The appropriate toys or play objects or materials can incite and enrich children's activities.

When choosing toys for young children, there are two main aspects that need to be considered. First is the hygienic/safety aspect. Toys must never endanger the health or physical well-being of the children. The second is the pedagogical aspect. Toys should be suitable and able to promote the child's interest. They should be open-ended, offering children an opportunity to engage with them in many different ways. As a result, children will play, with concentrated attention, for long periods, and in various ways.

For the youngest infants, we recommend a cotton scarf and objects that are easy to grab, protrude from the base, and do not roll (because some babies are nonmobile, they cannot go after a rolling object).

For babies at age six months, we recommend objects of various shapes, as they catch the children's attention and allow for tactile discoveries. These objects can be transferred from one hand to the other, be turned around with one or both hands, and also invite infants to manipulate them in various forms.

As children grow, they prefer objects of various sizes. They handle smaller objects (never small enough that they present a danger for accidents, i.e., they should not fit in their mouth, nose, or ears) with as much pleasure and interest as unusually larger ones, provided they can be manipulated.

Play activity is enriched with many new features during the second and third year of life. Play becomes more enriched by versatile, miscellaneous, and numerous toys. Gathering requires tubs, baskets, and building blocks containing several identical pieces that can be grouped and put into order according to color, shape, or size.

For the evolution of role-playing games, children need dolls and scarves that serve as blankets for the dolls. Wooden spoons, bowls, and cups become symbolic for feeding their dolls. Play clothes can invite them to act out various events in their own lives or imitate the role of an adult.

Whether toys can fulfill their pedagogical functions in a group also depends on their quantity. If there are not enough toys, part of the group is unable to play at their corresponding level, and the children who had access to the toys cannot play undisturbed either. There are ceaseless fights over the toys. There is no use in the caregiver explaining, asking, or intervening.

The only solution is the appropriate number of toys, which means that the number of objects should be several times the number of the children in the group. In order for each child to choose and decide what he wants to play with, it is not enough if there is only one object for each child in the group.

Without knowing the specifications of each environment, it is impossible to decide what quantity of objects to acquire for each group. If there is not enough space, it is not a good idea to further decrease the space with large toys. Financial aspects must also be considered. However, we must never, under any circumstance, give up on having enough basic toys (a bucket and a shovel for the sand pit or a doll or teddy bear) for each member of the group.

Toys are not luxuries. They are important tools for bringing up children and an essential material condition to support children's development."

Simple objects at the Pikler Institute offer unlimited possibilities for play and discovery. Photo by Marian Reismann from the Pikler archives.

Role of Caregiver During Children's Play

How does the adult internalize the importance of independent play? She does this by setting up the appropriate conditions for play, as well as letting children know that she is attentive and present during their play. Children want to be seen, and there is a relationship that happens between caregiver and child during play. Although not as intense as during caregiving interactions, children want to know that the adult sees him and is present to his discoveries. *"I see that you made a tall tower!"*

A caregiver with children during their outdoor play at the Pikler Institute. Photo by Maria Reismann from the Pikler archives.

A caregiver supports a child's developmental needs by setting the play space accordingly. One can begin by simply observing the child during his play and resisting the impulse to interrupt. While children are playing, her observations will give her cues on how to set up the environment the next day. These observations will also let her know the developmental stage of each child, his preferences for objects, and how they socialize with each other and learn to solve problems.

A space for infants will not be set up the same way as the space for older children. Infants will have things within reach because they are not yet mobile. Toddlers are offered the opportunity to move by having the toys arranged against the wall and on shelves. There are toys that will always be placed in the same spot and another that can be rotated. This creates a sense of mystery and discovery.

The toys are not hidden but are simply rearranged to bring new "life" to the objects. However, it is the caregiver's role to organize the space and tidy it up again when the children are napping or sleeping. It is pleasing for the eye to have order and an uncluttered environment.

The play objects should be suitable for the child's developmental stages and offer opportunities to be used in a variety of ways. Objects that are versatile enrich their play. Toys are an important part of children's development, as they support the child's well-being and offer him, for example, an opportunity to become a scientist learning about cause and effect, gravity, and other laws of physics.

Sporadically rearranging the environment and grouping smaller objects inside baskets or open containers can prevent chaos in the play space. This will also serve as an invitation for children to take things out and put them back, an important factor in the *collecting* stage of development.

There are times when conflict arises among children, when the adult needs to intervene. These situations may not always be easy for the caregiver, and that is why it is important that she is close by and available to support each situation accordingly. Children may also be able to problem-solve on their own.

However, when an intervention is necessary, a caregiver may say, *"There are other balls in that basket."* By letting the child know where he can find more toys or that she will assist him in finding another object, she is conveying her presence.

By being attentive to his ever-changing developmental needs, an observant caregiver will become skillful in anticipating and supplying children with the appropriate play materials.

Spontaneous role-play with caregiver at the Pikler Institute. Photo by Marian Reismann from the Pikler archives.

A new aspect of the importance of free playing and movement can be found in the following excerpt from Dr. Agnes Szanto-Feder's article, "Mutual Importance of Relationships and Motor Development[45]:

"Infants' movements have aroused an increasing interest among psychologists, including in those theories of Henri Wallon.[46] Indeed, for him, *movement is what can bear witness to the psychic life and expresses it entirely . . .*"

In the case of young children, this happens before they can speak.

Movement has two essential aspects. First, it is an expression: its direct role is to link the infant and his human surrounding. Second, it is present in the physical world: adaptation and means to know and master the environment in which the infant is going to live.

The infant's ability to manage and master his own movement in adequate conditions, and the place Pikler gives it in the everyday life is an example of the mutual influences between the caregiving relationship and the infant's movement.

We find ourselves at the meeting point of two streams of ideas of a pediatrician who tirelessly observed babies. The first one deals with the conditions in which the motor development happens, the second one deals with the infant's signals to which the adult can respond.

When the infant moves in his own way and in his own time, where each new stage or the use of what has been previously acquired is entirely because of his own initiative, an existing genetic programming is revealed. Furthermore, it has qualitative aspects: the movements are harmonious; the infant is at ease and masters his actions.

It, thus, becomes evident that the infant, through the intermediate stages, can be very active, he can be relaxed, and he doesn't need to strain and be clumsy.

---

45   Szanto-Feder, Agnes, "Una Mirada adulta sobre el niño en acción; El sentido del movimiento en la protoinfancia," EDICIONES CINCO, Buenos Aires, 2014, ch. 1, pp. 54–59.

46   Henri Wallon (1879–1962) was a French psychologist, theorist, and author primarily focused on child development.

The result is that the infant relaxes and has a feeling of security with regard to both his own actions and those of the adult. And through his ability to move when still very young (rolling, crawling, etc.), the infant can exercise initiatives that the adult can appreciate. Other initiatives are his wishes and his refusals, his early ability to anticipate, negotiate, and compromise his play initiatives (with all the motor elements, during a diapering for instance). For the adult, this contributes to making her consider the child as a partner instead of an object of the adult's activity.

The infant, moving with ease, confidence, self-assurance, and consciousness, shows a very keen sense of initiation and interest. In an adequate environment, he can find occasions for questions and discoveries completely autonomously. The richness of the activity, the infant's seriousness and assiduity, presents to the adult a continuous discovery.

It brings her a deep joy when she is ready to accept that the infant takes pleasure and joy in his own autonomy.

This is a fundamental element of a mutually respectful relationship. This respect is decisive in the moments of intimacy inasmuch as the adult takes seriously the manifestations or signals as well as the other more elaborate communication elements coming from a child who is otherwise calm and self-assured.

This respect is also decisive for the way the adult is naturally attentive to the conditions of the infant's environment that will allow him to move with pleasure and purposefulness, with ease and security, such as while discovering new things (toys, clothes, place, and furniture).

This is what develops from the relational content of what Pikler called autonomous activity. It provides a rich approach to understanding why it is not frustrating for the adult to let the infant initiate his own activity, particularly as far as movement is concerned. Instead, it brings her a deep joy by not making him do things that he is not yet ready to do. Above all, instead of prompting us to abandon the infant, it incites us to a more sustained attention and to a real dialogue.

Children of the Pikler Institute can be seen playing and moving freely in a number of Pikler films, including *A Baby's Attention at Play*; *Freedom to Move on One's Own*; *Playing, Activity, Thinking, Part 1 and Part 2*; *Babies and Young Children with Each Other*."

Chapter 2.7

The Right to Dignity and a Positive Image

All children have the right to be able to create a positive image of themselves.

Children's sense of belonging could be satisfied if the adults caring for them would take interest in getting to know them individually. For example, the caregiver may notice that the child has a particular preference for a play object and she makes a reference to it. *"This is the same teddy bear that you liked yesterday. You were playing with it before you went to take your nap."*

These allusions between past, present, and future help children become acquainted with time and space, as well as letting them know that someone cares about their special interests.

But how do I let the child know that I am proud of him or that I recognize his efforts? False praise can be detrimental for building self-esteem. We often hear in certain cultures the empty phrase "good job." Does this repeated phrase actually have a positive outcome?

When the child is looking at us to share his joy while playing, we can choose to say, *"I see you, you stacked the cups together"* or *"You reached the scarf, you had to stretch your arm really far."*

What would happen if every time we interact with a child, we treat him in a way that he feels he belongs? It is through our interactions and presence that we let children know how important they are to us.

What if we saw every interaction with each child as an opportunity for connection? A positive self-image of the child begins to form, and his relationship to himself blossoms in a way that will have lasting effects.

Can we turn our responsibility of caring for each young person into a respectful way of being together? Children long for a close relationship, and it is our choice as adults to offer it or not. We can often be mechanical in our care and in a hurry to get things done, or we can choose to be present, to slow down, and to be attentive to the child's cues, in order to elicit a deeper responsiveness.

By being fully present and attentive during our interactions, a child will come to trust the adult that cares for him and come to see the world as a beautiful place because all his needs are addressed. This directly correlates with how a child will come to feel about himself. The development of his positive self-image is crucial for his healthy emotional development.

What then happens is that children are respected and grow up to respect others. This virtuous cycle may play a key role toward creating a more peaceful world.

A little girl role-plays with her peer by gently combing her hair at the Pikler® Institute. Photo by Maria Reismann from the Pikler archives.

Role of the Caregiver in Supporting Children's Positive Self-Image

During their upbringing, children are often scolded for something they did wrong, and the negative behavior becomes the focus. This is especially dangerous in an institutional setting. For example, if the child disobeys a rule, and the adults in the institution scold him, he feels bad about himself and doesn't learn how he could have done things differently.

Instead, a professional needs to learn to control herself and not react immediately with a negative remark. For example, very often, almost the only thing the children hear are prohibitions, and the adult mostly talks to the child when he does something naughty, hurts another child, breaks a glass, etc.

"You did this wrong," "Don't chew this way," "Don't ask questions," "Don't bite," "Don't hit," etc. This is overwhelming for the child, and if the negative remarks continue over time, he will have a difficult time feeling good about himself.

When the child does something that is not allowed, we don't recommend judging the child. *"You are a bad child."* This would not support, in any way, his development of self-esteem. Instead, we recommend talking about the action and not the child himself.

It is important then to not judge the child but the action. We propose to focus on the action by saying, *"It is not safe to throw the cubes at the window, it can break"* or *"Those are the cloth diapers I washed this afternoon. They are hanging from this clothesline so they can dry. If they are pulled, they will fall back on the water, and I will have to wash them all over again."*

This removes shame and strengthens accountability for the action.

It is often the case in an institutional setting, however, to treat the child based on his negative behaviors. This is detrimental for the child's self-image because he constantly hears what a bad child he is. How can this ever be a good thing?

We need to change and begin addressing children with kindness. We can still set firm limits and boundaries but never by shaming and insults.

Our recommendation is to notice positive things that the child is doing throughout his day, focus on those positive aspects, and give him the feedback.

"Thank you for helping me pick up the toys," "Thank you for offering your arm so I can help you put on your sweater," or *"I see that you helped Luis find his teddy bear, thank you."*

However, often it is enough just to say *"Thank you."*

This communicates to the child that you share his joy and you are happy for the situation. A thank you is enough because it is self-evident. A lengthy explanation is not necessary.

This type of acknowledgment and positive affirmation strengthens empathy and a positive self-image. The child comes to see that his participation in the group matters and that he is an integral part of it.

In one of the lectures abroad, our colleague showed a film where children were eating. A participant asked her, *"What would you do if the children poured all the food out of the bowl?"*

The presenter was surprised at this question because this had never happened at Lóczy.

Because caregivers were not focused on the negative behaviors, the children learned to cooperate without needing to be defiant. They came to see cooperation as a pleasurable moment, where they felt good about themselves.

A group of children enjoying their meal together outdoors at the Pikler Institute. Photo by Maria Reismann from the Pikler archives.

Voice of Experience: Gabriela Tejeda[47]

When someone loves what he or she does, and it happens to involve children, this love grows and expands with every smile that accompanies big bright eyes telling you, "I did it!"

Children placed in children's homes have the same rights as those who grow up in a family nucleus. There is, however, a problem. With the busy hustle of the day-to-day life in a children's home, coupled with the limited staff training, these rights begin to get lost.

Raising children to have a healthy self-esteem becomes a complicated issue under these circumstances. The responsibility is no longer on the father or mother but on the group of caregivers in charge.

To be fair, as professionals, we must prepare ourselves with the same dedication that comes from being a parent. This devotion could help us guide them in other capabilities that include, but are not limited to, self-regulation, freedom of thought, and freedom of choice. These are essential for their development of self-esteem and having a positive self-image.

When we help rear a child that is confident and who has a positive image of himself, we keep him from at-risk behavior and the dangers that prevent him from growing into emotionally stable adults, meaning those who are capable of taking care of themselves and others when they choose to have a family.

Boosting a child's positive sense of himself involves greater challenges than merely aiding him in fostering self-esteem.

Children are born with a sense of awareness about themselves, one that increases with age. In other words, children demand attention and quickly learn how to get it. They solicit care and nourishment, and within months, they learn how to navigate and at times even adapt their modus operandi, depending on who is caring for them at any given time.

---

47   Gabriela Tejeda has been national director of VIFAC (VIDA EN FAMILIA) in Mexico since 2002. See CONTRIBUTORS page for her biography.

This could be why a caregiver, in turn, can be assured that a young child is calm while the one responsible for the next shift can express exactly the opposite. Children perceive love and respect according to how they are treated, and they interpret the actions of their caregiver either as love or aggression from their first days of life.

An eighteen-month old is already capable of exhibiting joy and pride or, sadly, even shame. Why then do we forget his right to build a positive and proud self-image, especially when he has his own consciousness and identity? Most children with typical development are cognizant of their actions and how these affect, for better or worse, their own well-being and environment.

This is why adults must encourage them to do things that make them feel good about themselves, avoiding situations where they feel shame, which, in turn, prevents them from building the positive self-image that they are entitled to.

From a very young age, children learn that their actions have consequences. They recognize the need for having achievable goals based on their own efforts. At the same time, they discover how to do or not do things in order to feel good about themselves, even when their goals were not reached.

To note their accomplishments, children formulate their wishes for personal improvement that then allow them to feel confident and empowered.

When a child has not reached his goal or feels unsatisfied with his results, his caregivers should make an effort, in an unobtrusive way, to encourage him to not give up and offer alternatives where he can experiment with other options for victory. This could be as simple as how the toys are arranged in the play area or allowing ample time for a meal to be enjoyed without him feeling rushed.

Another factor to consider with regard to children feeling loved and worthy of self-esteem is establishing adequate limits. Although we must respect a child's own pace, he must also know how far he can go with his own decision-making process. The caregiver should let the child know that under no circumstance will his safety be jeopardized.

The following are the ingredients for building a child's self-esteem:

- *Show them acceptance, their differences and limitations notwithstanding.*
- *Show respect and interest in their personal needs and individuality.*

This helps children view themselves as worthy individuals, allows them to advance in their own self-acceptance, and builds trust in the adult that cares for them. An attentive caregiver will know how to be with each child according to his unique needs and let him know how important he is in her life.

When we make a note of a child's positive behavior, he will attempt to repeat the good actions that led him to the validation he received. When the child is acknowledged, he comes to appreciate himself with higher regard than if we are constantly reprimanding him or pointing out his faults.

When children find pleasure in the success of their appropriate behavior, they begin steps toward building good habits that increasingly make them feel better about themselves. This also builds grit to help them recover from wrongdoings in order for them to continue to put forth an effort. With the adult's respect and acceptance, the child's self-esteem becomes even stronger.

Overprotection must be avoided but must never be confused with responding to a child's needs. His needs for food, hygiene, and loving care should never be compromised. And through every interaction, each child should always feel loved and respected by his caregiver.

It is important to offer a safe space where the child can explore and discover his environment where he can make decisions that will later lead to being able to dress himself, eat by himself, and develop a deeper collaboration in his care routines.

When children understand that we trust them, they will make an effort to do things as best they can. On the other hand, if we hinder their ability to succeed by their own accomplishments, they may feel paralyzed or risk going outside their comfort zone. It is the caregiver that will provide this foundation.

As caregivers that have been entrusted with the universe's most valuable treasure, we must offer children conditions to support their aspirations. We must also provide opportunities for them to explore and find satisfaction and help them develop tolerance when frustrated.

It is the responsibility of all, including the government, society, and each person involved in a child's life, to protect and accompany him through his harmonious development.

To help raise children into stable, productive adults, ones that are loving and capable of multiplying goodness, is a task for each person that has been fortunate to have, in her loving hands, the brightest stars of the universe: our children that live in children's homes.

Chapter 2.8

The Right to Be Respected and the Recognition of Ability

All children have the right to get support and respect for their individual rhythm of development.

Respect

David Elkind writes in his book *The Hurried Child: Growing Up Too Fast Too Soon*, "*The concept of childhood has become the unwilling, unintended victim of overwhelming stress—the stress borne of rapid, bewildering social change and constantly rising expectations . . . as a society, we have come to imagine that it is good for young people to mature rapidly. It is children's right to be children. In the end, a childhood is the most basic human right of children.*"[48]

Development is an integral part of children's lives. It is natural that everybody wants to see the child develop well, including parents and professionals. Certain medical data or statistics can help the adult get acquainted with milestones. This data can be presented as charts that dictate milestones to familiarize adults with approximately at what time the child can do what.

But the information presents averages, and the average doesn't denote that it is typical. It is just a mean. And it is a misunderstanding to believe that for a child to develop well, he will do exactly as the charts, showing the averages, dictate. Whether it's about movement, speech development, or becoming independent, children do not develop at the same rhythm. Our emphasis must be to respect his individual pace and help him develop in small steps. We do this by offering the proper conditions for him to move.

Not all children have to be able to stand up at the same age or eat independently at the same age. Children are often forced to learn what they are not mature enough to learn or do things that their bodies are

---

48 David Elkind, *The Hurried Child: Growing Up Too Fast Too Soon.* pp. 3, 221.

not yet ready to do. To sit up when they haven't even learned to roll from their backs to their tummies independently or to walk when they are just learning to crawl will only make them clumsy.

We do need to support a child within his own development so that he can be active at his own maturation level but not in a way that we impose a deadline that the child *must* meet. When a child is active and doesn't depend on the adult so much, and it is not the adult that puts him in a position that he cannot reach by himself, he is more confident in his free movement, resulting in even more independence and more activity.

In her book, *Give Me Time*, Pikler wrote, *"By letting the infant develop at his own rate, the baby chooses how to move, rather than being pushed to sit, stand, or walk before he is ready."* She emphasizes that a baby will learn how to solve problems when given the opportunity to take the initiative on his own.

Oftentimes, when a child is developing at a slower pace, he can be erroneously labeled without a proper diagnosis, as a child with atypical development, simply because he is reaching the milestones more slowly. However, when indeed there are children that need support from a physical or occupational therapist, the support is given by respectfully involving them in the process and never by force.

In institutions, there are many children with atypical development. This makes it more difficult for them to reach milestones as dictated by the charts, and they need more time to develop. Therefore, we should not be in a hurry for them to develop quickly.

In addition, when a baby is born prematurely or with a low birth weight (an infant born under 2,500 g, for example), the adults want the child to achieve all goals in same way as children with typical development. The truth is that he actually needs more time than children with typical development. Pikler found that children born with lower birth weights will develop at a slower rate but will eventually catch up.

In the following chart from the Pikler Institute, we can see the standard deviation of milestones for children with typical development and whose birth weight was over 2,500 g (based on data from 591 children.). And we can see that healthy children also reach the different stages at different times.

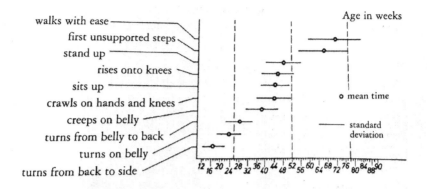

Chart edited by Elisa Rigol

The following is part of Pikler's findings:

Children with a birth weight of over 2,500 g mastered all movements before their peers. During the early stages of movement, the difference of mastery of milestones in the chart was a matter of only a week's difference. As the stages progressed, so did the difference in weeks. They became more pronounced toward the end of documented developmental stages, and there were substantial deviations in both directions: plus/minus four to six weeks difference for turning onto the side from the back; plus/minus twelve weeks difference for walking.

When Pikler and her colleagues examined the data of infants with a birth weight of 2,100 g to 2,500 g, they found a four to six weeks' difference on average, with the exception being when babies turn from their back onto their sides. This appeared to have a three-week difference.

For children weighing less than 2,000 g at birth, Pikler found that they tend to lag behind more than their normal birth weight peers, for example, turning onto their sides six weeks later. She also noted that they take their first steps approximately 17 weeks later than their peers.

When Pikler compared her findings with five other developmental charts,[49] she found that there were only two movements that children presented at a later time: returning onto back from the belly and standing up. Reasons for this may be the fact that, at Lóczy, children master on their own and without help each milestone. And turning belly to back only happens after baby has first mastered turning from back to belly.

The second movement is standing up. Her observations led her to believe that children at Lóczy have ample space to crawl and explore their safe environment. By not being kept in a crib, as was the case in most institutions, the children didn't need the urge to pull up from the bars to come to standing.

There are, as well, positions and movements observed at Lóczy that were not part of other developmental charts. Such is the case of kneeling, where children could actually play in this position or use as a form of locomotion before walking. Another difference is that the Lóczy children crawled before walking, not just horizontally, but also on stairs, slopes, and ladders. Pikler and her team deducted that these differences were because of the fact that the children were able to climb different surfaces. This does not tend to be the usual case in other institutions.

As we can see in these examples, children should never be hurried to master their milestones. Instead, we suggest supporting each child's unique developmental needs.

Here is another excerpt by Dr. Pikler[50]:

> "The independence, the feeling of competence of the child, is often checked by the way the adults are trying to help his development. The attitude by which the child is deprived from initiative under the pretext of "helping" and "teaching," from

---

49 Brunet/Lezine, 1951; Buehler/Hetzer, 1953; Gesell/Amatruda, 1964; Illingworth, 1960; Schmidt-Kolmer, 1958.

50 Pikler, Emmi, *The Competence of the Infant*, Acta Paediatrica Academiae Scientiarum Hungaricae, vol. 20 (2–3), 1970.

attempting things, andfrom completing an action he has started, should be revised. The so-called a bit of help i.e., *"I'll only just give him a hand to help him complete what he had begun,"* deprives the child from the joy of self-dependent achievement, from the feeling of efficacy, just like the traditional modes of helping, when the child is dealt with like an object.

A child whose rate of development is slower than usual in one or more areas is in particular danger. The slow performers are, as a rule, made to practice something for which they are not yet ready. The child is passively placed into the so-called more developed positions and is expected to perform more and more developed achievements.

He is asked to do things when he is not yet able to perform them by himself. Quite often sound and healthy children of a slower pace of development are in this way turned into helpless, clumsy, butterfingered ones.

Today we know that it is preferable to start school later than be always lagging behind in each class. It is better for everyone to realize his own abilities in an active, rich, many-sided way at his own standard, on his own level of development, than to be always lagging behind himself. This is increasingly true for infants and toddlers.

Teachers of young children and particularly theoretical specialists are seriously worried by the lack of initiative in children. The children prefer reproduction to invention, they prefer to imitate rather than to realize their own ideas. Small wonder, since they have been taught so ever since their early childhood.

In infants and young children, initiatives are suppressed; their inventive and experimental moods are stifled. Hence, the child's chances to achieve self-dependent initiatives, and to complete such initiatives, are restricted to closer and closer areas.

We must be aware of the importance of rearing infants and young children, of its effects upon their entire life. Like every other human activity, rearing and education should continually utilize the results of scientific research. The doctor's responsibility is particularly great, since, ultimately, it is the doctor whose instructions directly or indirectly determine the [adult's] attitude toward the undeveloped human being.

The doctor should not agree to follow harmful practices requiring reduced care but should instruct the adult to realize the importance of self-initiated motor activity; to not see infants solely as the subject of adult's activities, to whom she has to teach everything, but to see in the infant as an active partner.

If the doctor were to give sufficient attention to the child's competence, he could give rise to a major change in the rearing of infants and young children, which might prevent the appearance of many subsequent physical and somatic disorders.

By taking into account the infant's signals and initiatives, thus intensifying the infant's claims to competence, we could bring up calmer, more balanced children: children who would know more precisely what they are interested in and individually know their needs for food and sleep.

Their play and manipulation would be more independent; they would have a sound and active relationship to adults in general. A positive human tie grows out of mutual adaptation.

On the basis of such a relationship, the child's adjustment to society is a healthy process with fewer collisions than usual. His emotional life will be richer and more balanced, his social adjustment convenient. All this would eliminate the need for a number of subsequent corrective educational measures and would prevent many unnecessary somatic interventions and their consequences."

Respecting the child's own rhythm applies not only to his motor development, but also to speech development at different ages. They also differ from each other when they become independent in eating and in dressing themselves. In institutions, we often find children who have a difficult past, and these children usually develop more slowly than the average. Only when they feel secure and they have established affectionate relationships can they start their development in the different fields. This needs to be respected too.

Chapter 2.9

The Right to Family Contact and Support

All children have the right to know their personal history and to get support to stay in contact with their families.

As George Orwell once wrote, *"He who controls the past controls the future."* The philosophical question, *"Who am I?"* helps us understand our identity and its complexity. But in order to adequately answer this question, one must first know one's origins.

It is for this reason that we advocate for children knowing their personal history. This includes the child's history at the institute, his and his parents' personal history, and his ongoing contact with family. Because a child may arrive at a children's home without any information regarding his birth, his first few days, weeks, or months of life, the time spent in the nursery, will help establish his history.

From the moment he arrives at the nursery, it is crucial that the staff make a concerted effort to document this child's life in his personal diary. This will include his physical milestones, as well as the emotional and mental aspects of his development, adding to this any ailments or illnesses suffered and treatment received.

Photographs of the child in the group and during special celebrations are recommended. There should be written material of the child that he can take with him when he leaves the institute so that he doesn't lose the period of his life spent at the institute. There is an expression used in psychology, *"lost childhood,"* which means a period in the child's life that he doesn't remember. In a family, if a child doesn't remember, the parents will tell him stories, and together, they can remember.

However, this is not the case in an institution. The child's diary will give not only his personal history to the family or new home, but also to the child himself. As he grows older, he will be able to glance at this book and celebrate his history, without judgment—good or bad—but simply as recognition that this is *his* life.

When available, children need support to stay in contact with their natural family and be allowed to visit each other. Sensitivity is fundamental when speaking to the child about his family, and it should always be with integrity and ethics. No matter the situation, the child should never be told negative, or accusatory comments about his parents.

Family visit at the Pikler® Institute. Photo by Marian Reismann from the Pikler archives.

The time children spend in a residential nursery will have effects for the rest of their lives. For this reason, it is important that all caregivers and staff recognize the significance of their role in rearing infants in institutions. By giving them a pleasant and enjoyable beginning, they can grow up feeling good about themselves.

Myriam David wrote a poem titled "The Ten Commandments of Taking Care of Others' Children: A Plea from Worried Babies."[51] Originally in French, and from the perspective of children living in a children's home, David describes how a child asks for a pen and, on behalf of his peers and all children living in institutions, begins to write what he feels are the *ten commandments* that caregivers must respect.

He expresses to his caregiver the importance of never trying to be a substitute for his mother, the importance of understanding his body language, and the importance of taking care of him and how he will *love her for it.*

In his ninth commandment, he writes, *"If necessary, you will protect me from my mother and keep me away from her. But if so, you have to talk to me about it, explain it to me, and take me to meet her."* And in his tenth commandment, he writes, *"When we part, you will remember me, and I, the child you cared for so well, I will keep you in my heart, even if we never see each other again and I don't remember you very well."*

He signs it as coming from *The Federation of Babies.*

Wouldn't it be a lovely goal for every caregiver to have the children under her responsibility remember the good care she provided while honoring his personal history and for them to carry a positive memory of the time spent together? Memories felt in the heart and tied to a positive emotion live on.

---

51   David Myriam, "Soigner l'enfant d'autrui," érès, 1997.

András, based on an article by Éva Kalló.[52]

Kalló's written observations show that most children begin to mention their parents around the age of two.

During the first three years of living at the institute, there are usually no signs of children recognizing caregivers taking care of them, instead of their mothers and fathers. There is also no indication that children think they should be living with parents instead of at the institute.

The occasional meetings with parents are important and eagerly awaited events in their lives. The fact that a child's mother or father comes to visit only him and also brings him presents fills him with joy and pride, but he gives no signs of integrating his parents into future plans.

The child who is not visited does not seem to experience the absence of his parents as a deficit. It is sufficient for him to know that they exist. The intense longing for parents that is believed to embitter the child's life in institutions is not characteristic of a child at this age, if he is emotionally balanced and has a close and positive relationship with his caregivers.

Our experiences show that a child begins to understand his relationship to his parents after he has received answers from his caregivers about his birth and origin.

András's father visited him twice a month at most. Sometimes his grandmother came as well. His own mother visited only once, when András was nine months old. As with other children who are visited infrequently, András is uncomfortable during the visit, but afterward, he repeatedly speaks of his father with joy. He recalls what he was like and is noticeably disappointed if his father doesn't return again soon.

András tries to find excuses for his father's absence. He also expresses his anger by saying that his father is in the hospital because "his eyes have fallen out" and that's why he didn't visit. He also

---

52 Edited excerpt from Éva Kalló's "How a Child Living in an Infants' Home Meets His Past" article originally published in the Hungarian magazine *Esély* (*Chance*), 1993.

creates imaginary events in the past in which he is together with his father. "We had a bath together in the tub, my father and I," or "We caught a blackbird together."

In his fantasies, his mother appears once or twice: "My mummy and my daddy had dinner quickly and went to bed." At other times he speaks about his siblings or his unknown grandfather.

How can caregivers help children cope with their feelings? What kind of support do they receive from us in order to accept that others are going to raise them in place of their biological parents?

First of all, we help them by providing the necessary conditions and an atmosphere that allow them to feel that this is their home, a home where they are safe, where they can develop an intimate relationship with the least possible number of individually assigned caregivers, and where, in their relationships, they learn and experience a personal attachment of belonging to someone.

This makes them capable of developing new and deepening relationships with their adoptive or foster parents.

We can also help him by providing a story about life in the institute that consists of vivid memories and pleasant experiences long before he began to consider the question of birth. These stories include what he was like when he was small and how his caregivers saw him. For example, *"When you arrived, you were very little and lived in a different room," "When you started to sit on a bench at meals, you couldn't reach the ground with your feet, so we had to put a pillow under them,"* or *"Once, a long time ago, when you were sleeping in the garden, thunder woke you up, and you were very frightened. Your caregiver wrapped you in a blanket and ran into the room so that you wouldn't get wet."*

Regardless of whether the child remembers a more or less important event, whether he recalls joyful or painful experiences, in his memories, he has an image of himself as an important human being worthy of being loved.

This provides him with a personal history when the time comes for him to leave the institute. It is made up of events and memories shared with his caregivers. It gives him a past with which to build the future and which he will be able to refer to later.

But what can we do to create a place in his life story for his biological parents? How do we protect him from seeking relief in dreams and constructing idealized pictures of parents or, more importantly, from hating them?

When András's father no longer visited, the caregivers didn't try to reassure him by saying that he would come again. They listened to the excuses he found to account for his father's absence without either confirming or denying them, in order not to raise false hopes. They showed understanding for his despair and expressed their own desire for his father to come again. But they told him that they did not know his father, nor why he didn't come.

Listening to the stories he made up, they took care not to confront him with their improbability. Without rejecting his fantasies, they talked with him about the real details of his father's visits. This was an attempt to help András remember his father later, when he would no longer be able to recall what he looked like but could repeat what he had heard from his caregivers about him and about his visits.

As time passed, there was less and less hope of András seeing his father again. Although he talked about him and would still like to see him, his words gradually lost their emotional charge. *"I live here, and I am not going home with my father,"* he said one day.

This sentence expressed both the lost hopes and the acceptance of reality.

He was four years old when he finally left the institute, happily holding the hand of his adoptive mother. We gave her a detailed description of András's life and development, which was based on the notes the caregivers had kept in his diary. He took the toys he got for Christmas and for his birthday, as well as the small car his father had given him. He also took a photo album with a picture of his caregiver.

Voice of Experience: Intisar Shareef, EdD[53]

When I reflect on what I think I know about any particular subject, I'm often reminded that I must examine whatever I know against who I am. My perspectives about the world are totally related to my perspectives about myself. When did I form opinions about my being? It was before I was ever aware that such opinions were even my own.

In other words, we are formed by others.

So one's personal history is the foundation of one's notion about everything. That personal history was forming before birth. Sounds were heard, maternal heartbeat was felt, smells registered. Although primitive, we were born with a history and a knowledge of self and others. This inborn intelligence and connection is a right we must honor and respect.

When children are separated from their birth families, an essential part of their being is compromised. Some professionals in the adoption field refer to this loss connection as a primal wound. If we truly believe the connection existed in the beginning of life, then we must do something to help the child heal and remain attached in some way to their origins.

Setting aside adult agendas and needs and seeking to support the best interest of the child will lead us to higher ground in our decision-making. There is no "one size fits all" or one "right answer" to this dilemma. However, the informed and developed consciousness of adults who truly believe in the intelligence and well-being of children will guide us to every opportunity to connect the child to his or her roots.

Describing exactly that seems impossible. There are too many variables. Some children may benefit from being parented by two families; some may simply want to know the facts about their birth families and the circumstances that separated them. Others may

---

53 Dr. Intisar Shareef is department chair of early childhood education at Contra Costa College in San Pablo, California. See CONTRIBUTORS page for her biography.

just want to talk about their birth parents and have their questions answered honestly.

Most don't want or need our judgments about any of this. Again, there are so many variations on the theme. However, one thing is certain: children want and need to know something. Where did they come from? Who are their people? What is their story? The adult response to these questions will shape the child's perspective of the world. We must respond with thoughtfulness and courage.

One initial step that caregivers can take is a commitment to honesty. Taking a self-inventory, acknowledging one's own needs and fears, and working on oneself enables the adult to come into the life of a child with less "baggage." Lightening one's personal load will enable the adult to have and to hold space for the child.

Tell the child his or her story in age-appropriate ways and accept that the telling acknowledges loss and that loss brings grief. Help children move through grief at their own pace. Difficult? You bet, but what a gift the child receives when they learn they can love all the people who are responsible for their existence.

When children feel supported to love freely and to connect openly and honestly to the people they identify with, they are given a freedom to be authentically themselves. People who feel good about themselves most often feel good about others.

This, I believe, is a blueprint for a peaceful world.

Chapter 2.10

The Right to a Secure and Loving Family

All children should have the right to be helped in finding a beneficial solution to live in a loving family.

Transition

The goal of nursery homes should be to provide all the necessary conditions for children to develop a healthy personality, a positive image of themselves, and an optimistic view about the world. This will allow them to adapt to the family they will grow up in. It is important that from the moment a child is admitted into an institution, it considers what will be the best possible situation for the child's future: returning to birth family, foster care, or adoption.

It is not always easy to prepare a child for the transfer between the children's home and his new family home. This transition requires time and forethought, keeping the child's adaptability and best interests in mind. It is a common misconception to think that immediately placing a child in his new home is the best solution.

However, if a child is removed and placed in a new home without any preparation, it can cause him insecurity and disorientation. There are a series of gentle steps that could be implemented to ease his transition and making it an easier process.

The family needs to know about the child's life during the time he spent at the institution. The child's personal diary plays a key role. By keeping a diary and records of the child, the family would receive details about all the aspects of the child's physical and socio-emotional development. Personal habits, preferences for foods or toys, and who his friends were will also shed a deeper light into the child's temperament. In addition to the family learning about the child with more detail, the diary will later help the child remember his personal history during his stay at the infants' home.

During the phase of becoming acquainted with parents, the child should be first made aware of what is happening and of any future changes that will be occurring in his life after leaving the children's home. Depending on the child's age, becoming acquainted can be that parents become involved during caregiving routines or have the opportunity of playing together.

In the beginning, the caregiver's presence provides a sense of security to the child, as she becomes a bridge between the two. (In the case of the child being transferred to another institute, the same transition would apply with the new staff.)

To further ease the transition of settling into a new home, children must take with them all the objects that belong to them and are part of their personal belongings. These include items of clothing that they own, their own toys, transitional object that they use for sleeping, their personal photo album, and anything else that they have been gifted during their stay at the children's home. These will serve as a tool between past, present, and future.

When we met with Tünde Kertész (whom we spoke about in Right One), she brought along her photo album from her six years living at Lóczy and was eager to show it to us. This signified the importance of her photo book and how instrumental it had been for her to have her first six years of life documented. The pages, filled with pictures of herself and other happy infants and young children, included commentary from her lead caregiver, who added handwritten notes and relevant information about each photo. This special book holds a key to her personal history.

Indeed, with Kertész, who leafed through her personal photo book with us, it was apparent that the young woman with the gentle voice and dignified demeanor took immense pride in both her past and her present.

Tünde sharing her photo book with Elsa Chahin. Photo by Alex Kajtar.

Voice of Experience: María Vásquez[54]

Institutions in charge of the care and legal process of the child have the important decisive role of the child's life and society. Understanding and responsibly assuming the need to create the conditions that will allow the child to achieve significant and transcendental experiences is a priority. A very important aspect as well is finding the ideal families and sharing with them the importance of loving care.

Any human act that sets aside or delays the need for love provokes fatal consequences for life on our planet. Without love, we lose perspective of growth, sensitivity, creativity, solidarity, and respect. Its absence causes great suffering and gives way to inexplicable expressions of abuse, control, authoritarianism, war, and self-destruction. Therefore, a child belonging to an affectionate family is a vital requirement for human development and serves as the foundation for self-awareness.

Children need unconditional love and can only integrate it if it is tangible, concrete, and palpable. Physical contact is essential. It can be expressed through purposeful hugs, delicate words, and gentle touch. The adult's attentive gestures and movements during body-care routines invite the child's active participation.

To offer unconditional love to children does not mean letting them do whatever they want. That would be a form of neglect. The child must always be able to count on unconditionally loving support, especially during difficult times. These can include a lack of clarity in his feelings or thoughts when expressing discomfort and when faced with unsuitable experiences.

The child gives many signs when he is unwell, with these signs running the risk of being misinterpreted by the adult. Undertaking a loving responsibility of respect with children prevents adults from resorting to excessive and authoritarian demands that can lead children to act out with defense mechanisms.

54　We share more about María Vásquez and her organization in Ecuador, Casa Ami, in part three. See CONTRIBUTORS page for her biography.

By choosing to support the child's process, adults have the opportunity to grow with him and to understand him more and more. It becomes possible to attune to important moments in the relationship, for example, when the child needs something from the adult. A sensitivity to not interfere with the children's activities can also evolve, as well as when and how to set limits tenderly and decisively.

Once these foundations are established within a family, all members can live peacefully and be present to one another's needs. A loving family can very well be the biological or an adoptive family, inclusive of differences (cultural or of any other nature).

The family has the responsibility to safeguard the child's physical and mental health, to support their emotional balance, and to favor the necessary conditions that will allow the child to adapt to existing global realities without losing himself.

Life in a Family

When children grow up in an institution, they need to feel like they are part of a family. Their group *is* their family. This type of belonging prepares a child for when he is later integrated into a family setting.

At times living conditions of the birth family may change during the child's life at the institute, offering him a better opportunity for optimal development in his own home. When this is the case, children should be supported to return to their birth families. However, in other situations, where the birth families do not have contact with the child, foster care or adoption are imminent.

There are many babies in the world needing a home. And there are many loving adults that would like to receive them and form a family. By preparing children to be part of a group, they will have an easier time adapting and finding an attachment figure in a mother or father.

Becoming a foster or adoptive parent is a big decision and commitment. The rewards can be filled with joy, as both child and parent are making a difference in each other's lives. Unfortunately, it is not always an easy journey for all involved. Sometimes the adoption process may take years, postponing the dream of their new life together.

The journey is not easier as a foster family. Foster parents will need to respect that sometimes the child will need to go back to his biological family. And although there is that understanding from the beginning, it doesn't make it any less painful. Emotions and feelings of attachment are now involved.

Our next voice of experience speaks about a mother's love. It is the love story between Caroline and Ever that inspires us and validates our belief that there is, indeed, so much love to be offered to our vulnerable young.

Voice of Experience: Caroline Wilcox, MA[55]

I am a Los Angeles County foster and adoptive parent, and I always knew that I wanted to be a mom, but I did not know how my path to parenthood would define me. There were over 30,000 children in Los Angeles County foster care who needed a parent, so I took classes, passed the financial and medical reviews, set up a kid's room, had my home inspected, and became a licensed foster parent.

In the summer of 2011, I got the call that would change my life: A nine-month-old girl had been found locked in a closet during a drug raid. The baby's parents were gang members who had already lost an older child to the system, and my social worker told me the case looked like it could lead to adoption.

It was the Fourth of July weekend, and soon Baby A was placed in my arms. I instantly fell in love with her and spent the next year doing everything I could to make Baby A feel safe and loved. But unlike most new moms, I also had to supervise visits with her biological family in jails, rehab facilities, and DCFS (Department of Children and Family Services) offices across the county.

---

55 Caroline Wilcox is an educator who, for the last sixteen years, has taught upper elementary school. See CONTRIBUTORS page for her biography.

A year later, Baby A was reunited with her biological parents, and I didn't know how I would survive giving up this child that I loved. But I also knew that this was what I had signed up for. As the adult, I should carry all the risk and heartbreak, if it could possibly protect Baby A, and make her feel loved and safe during the worst moments of her young life.

Three months later, my social worker said she came across a fifteen-month-old girl who was legally free for adoption but had been declared "failure to thrive." This meant that she was not growing or developing properly, and she had been returned to the system on multiple occasions.

I met with medical professionals and social workers before making a decision. More ailments were laid out before me (she held her breath until she passed out and had seizures, she refused to eat or drink and had significant GI disorders, among others).

My gut told me everything could be environmental, but since I was a mom without a baby, and this baby needed a mom, I said yes. As I left the office, the social worker told me to think of a new name so she could start fresh without any negative associations. I never thought I would be able to name my child as an adoptive foster mom, but I knew her name instantly—Ever.

A few days later, Ever was dropped off, and within six months, the little girl who would not drink, eat, or bond was doing all those things, as well as meeting most of her developmental milestones.

A year later, a social worker sat in my living room doing our annual home study while Ever played, frequently coming over to "give me love" or chatter about what she was going to feed her doll. The worker asked how Ever was doing with another child in the house.

After a few minutes, we realized his mistake: He could not reconcile the healthy, happy, and engaged child before him with the child detailed in the file on his lap, assuming she must have been another child.

It is astonishing how quickly unconditional love, security, and nutrition can transform a child and bring out her strengths and talents. At five, Ever is bright, socially aware, independent, and as loving and empathetic as a child can be.

My experiences toughened me up and gave me the strength and the hunger to parent a little one with a heartbreaking history. Fostering and adopting is not the right fit for everyone, but if you have love to give, there are over half a million children in the United States' foster care system ready to receive it.

A poem to Ever.

Dear Ever,

I have been dreaming about you, and now I know your name. You have been blessed with the precious gift of life; and as your fire ignites, another flickers out. Here you are now, waiting to be loved. You will come to know this feeling of love because, in essence, you are love.

Can I hold you? Would you like for me to hold you? I ask you with respect, because this is what you deserve. My excitement and emotions interfere with your calmness, so I take a breath and slow down to adapt to your pace. I can pick you up when you are ready, and by reading your cues, I can know when it is time for me to embrace you tenderly, securely.

My hands may represent the beginning of your world. My hands will tell you how I feel about you, so I need not hurry them. As I support your spine, your equilibrium is not perturbed, you can relax and be comfortable, open to enjoying the experience.

I feel you in my arms and the whole world stands still. There is a moment of communion between the two of us, a feeling of oneness. Yes, Ever, sweet angel, we are one. Do you feel it too? As I bring you close to my heart, you recognize the rhythmic repetition, the same vibration that for nine months enveloped your world.

You relish in the recognition of this familiarity. I can almost hear your coos as you snuggle closer. Boom-boom, boom-boom, and you are soothed, boom-boom, boom-boom, you feel connected: You feel loved. Your eyes meet mine for the first time, and jointly, we exhale a sigh of relief. We are together. A relationship is being born and you begin to trust.

I am with you, so there is no need to feel alone. You are special, as all babies and all children are special. Sometimes we adults forget that your world, as a baby, is commencing, and what we transmit in those early stages will become the connections you create in your brain, affecting you throughout your life.

I want to care for you tenderly so that your experiences are positive and can prepare you for a future of fulfillment. Your sense of self is developing. You are forming the image of yourself. Our interdependence will be nurturing, inviting you to have faith in your importance in this world.

As you grow and develop, Ever, respect will become a familiar word and a recognizable feeling that you cannot do without. You will excel in love. Give thanks for the precious gift of having been born, as I too give thanks for the realization of the dream of calling you my daughter. Let us grow happy together.

Your adoptive mother,

Caroline

Chapter 2.11

Children with Special Needs

All ten rights also pertain to children with special needs, which is why we found it important to add a chapter about this topic.

Our role with children with special needs is to ensure their day-to-day joys and not just to focus on what these children cannot do. It is important to offer individual attention and support according to their unique developmental rhythm. Every child deserves the opportunity to get to know his own abilities and be emotionally taken care of.

It is not about what we choose to communicate with children but *how* we communicate it. In essence, it is all about *how* we are with the child. During caregiving interactions as well as in occupational-therapy sessions, we must ensure that the child is always acknowledged and given time to adapt to what we are asking of him.

The Piklerian principles were formulated in relation to the development of healthy infants and toddler. In the course of its history, more and more children with special needs found their home at the Pikler Institute by order of the Hungarian government. It was this reality that motivated Pikler's colleagues to think about how the Piklerian principles could be combined with the special educational principles.

An important step in this direction was presented by Dr. Sjoukje Borbély (in a film by Borbély and Szentpétery[56]). The search for a solution continues, as the subtitle of the film explains, *Special Education within Lóczy Is an Interesting Challenge*.

The question raised here is, *how* can the Piklerian approach and special education support each other for children with slow or different developmental needs? In other words, how can special education contribute to the Piklerian approach, and what can the Piklerian approach add to the special education?

---

56 Dr. Sjoukje Borbély: Special Education within Lóczy and Dr. Sjoukje Borbély – Borbála Szentpétery: *Children with Special Needs Living in Lóczy—An Interesting Challenge*, (www.pikler.hu and https://pikler.org).

Excerpt by Dr. Sjoukje Borbély[57]

"Children with special needs require additional support. It is not a coincidence that children living with a handicap have now widely been referred to as children with special needs, instead of children with hindrances.

In the cases of children living with disabilities, the dilemmas of social integration are present on multiple levels. They do not concern only the future, but also the here and now; and they are not only of social, but also of a therapeutic nature. If we neglect the challenges that children with special needs face, we would not be able to create the optimal framework that would enable them to become integral members of their group, endangering their socialization in the here and now . . .

However, the art of providing special assistance to children with special needs growing up in Lóczy was doubly difficult. It could not happen at the expense of the other children. So there was a need to search for answers to the questions arising from these dilemmas.

Can the role of the caregiver change when she is taking care of a disabled child?

Without certain information, the caregiver may take care of a child with special needs merely as if he were a younger child, but this approach is not right. Slower development also means different development. The caregiver must be aware of what individual problems are or what inadequate unfolding of certain functions means, from the perspective of the overall development. She must receive help in order to optimally communicate with the child in question in spite of the problem . . .

The goal is achieving optimal communication, with a sequence of actions, while introducing changes gradually, is also very important.

---

57 Dr. Sjoukje Borbély, *Special Education within Lóczy*, accompanying booklet to the film by Dr. Sjoukje Borbély – Borbála Szentpétery: *Children with Special Needs Living in Lóczy—An Interesting Challenge.*

The pedagogical situation, the fact that the care is predictable for the children, absolutely fulfills the special therapeutic principles. So the dilemma is only in providing more support to the caregivers. This can be, for example, in the case of children who are not chewing, not holding their cup, and seemingly not cooperating on the diaper-changing table, by helping them do what they already can, perhaps in slower steps or by different measures. The sequence of the smaller steps, however, is never mixed up or changed.

If a child does not develop well during care, in spite of the existing system, a special therapist is brought in to diagnose and give advice; based on the personality and individual characteristics of the child already examined from several aspects by that time, [the advice is given] on what kind of hindrances and internal integration, as well as coordination problems may be causing communication dilemmas.

Their special needs must be recognized and satisfied."

The following is an edited conversation between Szentpétery[58] and Chahin:

I have learned at Lóczy, as an occupational therapist, that coming to know the child is the base of the cooperation and that the support we offer them must be based on our objective observations. Diagnoses don't always show us the areas in which the children can actually follow their own activities. The more one observes children, the more one can find out which topics or areas they are interested in and where they can have their own initiative.

By keeping track of each child's individual development through continued observations, one can arrive at concrete solutions,

---

58 Borbála Szentpétery is an occupational therapist who worked at the Pikler residential nursery, currrently works at the Pikler Daycare Center as a pedagogue in the play room, and leads Pikler® parent/child groups. See CONTRIBUTORS page for her biography.

respectively. And by offering challenges that he can tackle during play, he can discover new possibilities on his own.

At the Pikler Institute, we don't start from data. "This child is xx old, so he must be doing this by now, reaching certain milestones, etc." Instead, we observe where he is at in his development. By observing each individual, we cannot offer a universal recipe or "one size fits all" approach. Each intervention is uniquely designed to meet each child's needs, taking into account his personal interests.

But how does a therapist present activities to a child where he feels like engaging in them? A concrete tool that we incorporate includes giving the child more time. Based on the knowledge of the course of development of typical children, we provide more time and more practicing opportunities for children with special needs.

Repetition requires time.

There are times, however, when the child cannot move on from an activity. Because his mental focus is quite narrow, he feels comfortable with repeating the same thing over and over and over again. How long the therapist offers the opportunity for repetition and when it is time to intervene by presenting a new idea or a new activity depends on the relationship that exists between the two. The knowledge of the child will guide us when to say, "You can keep practicing," or, "It's time to move on."

The goal is to help him broaden his scope and develop self-confidence.

Another tool is creating an appropriate environment with toys that will invite children to engage in an activity. In the case of children whose attention wanders off topic easily and gets distracted, we can set up the environment where they can focus on what we want them to focus on. If too many objects are crammed in, it will not be easy for them to focus on one thing. Or if we see that a specific object doesn't captivate the child's attention, we need to find one that will.

A third tool has to do with our own presence and patience in order that we can share in the child's pleasure.

Occupational therapy was offered twice a week at Lóczy. Our sessions were not necessarily based on the clock, and they lasted from twenty minutes to one hour, depending on the child's need. It was important, though, that his sessions were linked to one of his daily routine activities, for example, sessions were scheduled before the meal or after the afternoon snack.

The first time Sjoukje was my supervisor, she visited once in a fortnight. Working with a boy with a severe physical disability, we developed a ritual. The caregiver gave me this boy in my arms. This transition helped him feel safe. While we went to the therapy room, we looked at different objects, stopping at whatever interested him. This offered a sense of predictability and anticipation. He turned out to be interested in things that moved, and I offered him space to interact with plants, the picture frames on the wall, or the curtains in front of the window.

Sometimes I tried to introduce him to the idea that parting the curtains could also lead to looking out to the garden, but it was the moving of the curtain that was more interesting for him. Once when I put him onto the floor, he still wanted to play with the curtains. He surprised me when he unexpectedly stood up in order to continue playing with the curtains, although he never stood up on his own before, but he was three years and eight months old.

His confidence and independence soared by following his interest.

There was another boy living at Lóczy from birth to age seven. He was born with femur aplasia (underdevelopment of the thigh bones), and despite the odds, he learned to walk, which is not a typical outcome.

Early on, he demonstrated a certain fascination for numerical calculations, time, and watches. At one of the parties when he was in kindergarten, he even dressed up as a clock. (He still lived at Lóczy but was attending kindergarten in the neighborhood.) By knowing his interests, we were able to support him accordingly, by providing the proper elements.

As soon as he began living with his foster family, he learned how to play chess and loved it, and then he had the opportunity to join a chess club. Noticing his enthusiasm for the game, his coach decided to nominate him to participate in competitions. Now he plays regularly in tournaments and championships and has won many trophies. I have kept in touch with him and his foster family, and it happened that his foster mother asked me to be present at one of his championships.

What I learned from the late Éva Kálló, author and teacher of the Piklerian principles, about children with typical development has helped my work with children with special needs. It is about the relationship, about the bond between the child and the adult. In this relationship, the child, during his caregiving interactions, as well as in his self-initiated activities (including play and gross motor development), should be given as much freedom, not less and not more, as he can responsibly handle.

Borbála Szentpétery during a therapy session at the Pikler Institute. Photo from the cover of the booklet *Special Education within Lóczy, An interesting challenge*, Hungarian Pikler- Lóczy Association.

PART THREE

A person is a person through other persons. None of us comes into the world fully formed. We would not know how to think, or walk, or speak, or behave as human beings, unless we learned it from other human beings. We need other human beings in order to be human. I am because other people are. A person is entitled to a stable community life, and the first of these communities is the family.

—Desmond Tutu

SOME EXPERIENCES AND IDEAS
FROM AROUND THE WORLD

A children's home becomes the child's family during his stay and is the foundation that he will carry with him throughout his life. We have an opportunity to make it a joyful and loving experience for them.

In this next section, we present voices of colleagues from around the world that have made a difference in implementing good practices of care with children or have benefitted from them. Their dedication and determination to improving the lives of children living in children's homes transcends cultural barriers. Their humanity and purpose not only inspires us, but also offer us hope.

Chapter 3.1

It is our moral obligation to give every child the very best education possible.

—**Desmond Tutu**

Study Finds Orphanages Are Viable Options for Some Children
Case Study, Duke University[59],[60]

By Whetten, K.; Ostermann, J.; Whetten, R. A.; Pence, B. W.; O'Donnell, K.; Messer, L. C.; Thielman, N. M. The Positive Outcomes for Orphans (POFO) Research Team

DURHAM, NORTH CAROLINA—A Duke University study of more than 3,000 orphaned and abandoned children in five Asian and African countries has found that children in institutional orphanages fare as well or better than those who live in the community.

These findings contrast sharply with research that associates institutions with poorer health and well-being and the policies adopted by many international agencies/governments.

"Our research is not saying that institutions are better. What we found is that institutions may be a viable option for some kids," said study leader Kathryn Whetten, director of the Center for Health Policy at the Duke Global Health Institute.

As the number of orphans continues to rise worldwide, it is vital not to discount orphanages before assessing whether they are harmful to the millions of children for whom they care.

---

59 Duke GLOBAL HEALTH INSTITUTE, December 17, 2009. Whetten, K.; Ostermann, J.; Whetten, R. A.; Pence, B.W.; O'Donnell, K.; Messer, L. C.; Thielman, N. M. The Positive Outcomes for Orphans (POFO) Research Team. (2009). A comparison of the well-being of orphans and abandoned children ages six through twelve in institutional and community-based care settings in five less wealthy nations. *PLoS One*, 2009 December 18;4(12):e8169. PMCID: PMC2790618. doi: 10.1371/journal.pone.0008169.

60 See CONTRIBUTORS page for Dr. Whetten's biography.

Whetten's research team compared the physical health, cognitive functioning, emotion, behavior, and growth of orphaned or abandoned Children ages six through 12, half of them living in institutions and the other half dwelling in the community. The study found that children in institutions in five countries reported significantly better health scores, lower prevalence of recent sickness, and fewer emotional difficulties than community-dwelling children. These findings suggest the overall health of children in orphanages is no worse than that of children in communities.

The research team has been following the 3,000 orphans involved in the study for three years, and they plan to continue tracking them into their late teens and early twenties to determine how their childhood affects their life course.

Published in December 2009, in the interactive open-access journal *PloS ONE*, this is one of the most comprehensive studies of orphans ever conducted. Data was collected between May 2006 and February 2008 from children and their caregivers in 83 institutional care settings and 311 community clusters.

The study assessed five culturally, politically, and religiously distinct countries that face rising orphan populations. Sites included Cambodia, Ethiopia, Hyderabad and Nagaland in India, Kenya, and Tanzania.

"Very few studies cross a span of countries like ours does," said Whetten. "The design flaw of past studies is that they compared a small number of orphanages against community houses. Those limited results can't be generalized to other places."

Some of the most influential studies on child institutions were conducted in eastern bloc countries. But the greatest burden of orphans and abandoned children is in sub-Saharan Africa and Southern and Southeastern Asia.

Of the estimated 143 million orphans and abandoned children worldwide, roughly half reside in South and East Asia, according to UNICEF. An estimated 12% of all children in Africa will be orphaned by next year as a result of malaria, tuberculosis, pregnancy complications, HIV/AIDS, and natural disasters, according to the World Health Organization.

The Duke study included less formal institutions in Asia and Africa that were not studied before and not easily recognized. Researchers spent the first six months meeting with members of each community to identify and map orphanage locations. In Moshi, Tanzania, the research team found 23 orphanages after initially learning of just three from local government officials.

"What people don't understand is that, in many cases, the institutions are the community's response to caring for orphaned and abandoned children," said Whetten. "These communities love kids, and as parents die, children are left behind. So the individuals who love children most and want to care for them build a building and that becomes an institution.

"These institutions do not look or feel like the images that many in this country have of Eastern bloc orphanages. They are mostly places where kids are being loved and cared for and have stable environments."

The research findings run contrary to global policies held by children's rights organizations, such as UNICEF and UNAIDS, which recommend institutions for orphaned and abandoned children only as a last resort and urge that such children be moved as quickly as possible to a residential family setting.

"This is not the time to be creating policies that shut down good options for kids. We need to have as many options as possible," said Whetten. "Our research just says 'slow down and let's look at the facts.' It's assumed that the quality of caregiving is a function of being institutionalized, but you can change the caregiving without changing the physical building."

Whetten added that more studies are needed to understand which kinds of care promote child well-being. She believes successful approaches may transcend the structural definitions of institutions or family homes.

"Let's get beyond labeling an institution as good or bad," Whetten said. "What is the quality of care inside that building and how can we help the community identify cost-feasible solutions that can be delivered in small group homes, large group homes, and family homes?"

The study was supported by grants from the National Institute of Child Health and Development. Other Duke researchers involved in the study include Rachel Whetten, Jan Ostermann, Nathan Thielman, Karen O'Donnell, Brian Pence, and Lynne Messer.

PLoS One: "A Comparison of the Well-Being of Orphans and Abandoned Children Ages 6 to 12 in Institutional and Community-Based Care Settings in 5 Less Wealthy Nations."

References:

Gray, C.L.; B. W. Pence; L. C. Messer; J. Ostermann; R. A. Whetten; K. O'Donnell; N. M. Thielman; K. Whetten, and The POFO Study Team. Civic engagement among orphans and non-orphans in five low- and middle-income countries. Globalization and Health. 12(1):61. 2016. **DOI:** 10.1186/s12992-016-0202-8

Gray, C.L.; Whetten, K.; Messer, L. C.; Whetten, R. A.; Ostermann, J.; O'Donnell, K.; Thielman, N. M.; Pence, B. W. (2016). Potentially traumatic experiences and sexual health among orphaned and separated adolescents in five low- and middle-income countries. *AIDS Care,* 2016 March 2:1-9. PMCID: PMC4917905. doi: 10.1080/09540121.2016.1147013.

Sinha, A.; Lombe, M.; Saltzman, L. Y.; Whetten, K.; Whetten, R. Positive Outcomes for Orphans Research Team. (2016). Exploring Factors Associated with Educational Outcomes for Orphan and Abandoned Children in India. *Global Social Welfare*, 3(1):23–32. PMCID: PMC4830269. doi: 10.1007/s40609-016-0043-7.

Gray, C. L.; Pence, B. W.; Ostermann, J.; Whetten, R. A.; O'Donnell, K.; Thielman, N. M.; Whetten, K. (2015). Prevalence and incidence of traumatic experiences among orphans in institutional and family-based care settings in five LMIC: A longitudinal study. *Global Health Science and Practice*, 2015 August 25. PMCID: PMC4570014. doi: 10.9745/GHSP-D-15-00093.

Gray, C. L.; Pence, B. W.; Ostermann, J.; Whetten, R.; O'Donnell, K.; Thielman, N. M.; Whetten, K. (2015). Gender (in)differences in prevalence and incidence of traumatic experiences among orphaned and separated children living in five low- and middle-income countries. *Global Mental Health, 2*:e3. PMCID: PMC4467827. doi: 10.1017/gmh.2015.1.

Whetten, K.; Ostermann, J.; Pence, B. W.; Whetten, R. A.; Messer, L. C.; Ariely, S.; O'Donnell, K.; Wasonga, A. I.; Vann, V.; Itemba, D.; Eticha, M.; Madan, I.; Thielman, N. M. Positive Outcomes for Orphans (POFO) Research Team. (2014). Three-year change in the well-being of orphaned and separated children in institutional and family-based care settings in five low- and middle-income countries. *PLoS One,* 2014 August 27; 9(8):e104872. PMCID: PMC4146542. doi: 10.1371/journal.pone.0104872.

Escueta, M.; Whetten, K.; Ostermann, J.; O'Donnell, K. The Positive Outcomes for Orphans (POFO) Research Team. (2014). Adverse Childhood Experiences, Psychosocial Well-Being and Cognitive Development among Orphans and Abandoned Children in Five Low-Income Countries. *BMC International Health and Human Rights,* 2014 March 10; 14:6. PMCID: PMC3975306. doi: 10.1186/1472-698X-14-6.

Rajan, D. G.; Shirey, K.; Ostermann, J.; Whetten, R.; O'Donnell, K.; Whetten, K. (2013). Child and caregiver concordance of potentially traumatic events experienced by orphaned and abandoned children. *Vulnerable Children and Youth Studies: An International Interdisciplinary Journal for Research, Policy and Care,* 2014; *9(3)*:220-233. PMCID: PMC4217223. doi: 10.1080/17450128.2013.855346.

Thielman, N.; Ostermann, J.; Whetten, K.; Whetten, R.; O'Donnell, K. Positive Outcomes for Orphans Research Team. (2012). Correlates of poor health among orphans and abandoned children in less wealthy countries: the importance of caregiver health. *PLoS One,* 7(6):e38109. PMCID: PMC3374817. doi: 10.1371/journal.pone.0038109.

O'Donnell, K.; Murphy, R.; Ostermann, J.; Masnick, M.; Whetten, R. A.; Madden, E.; Thielman, N. M.; Whetten, K. Positive Outcomes for Orphans (POFO) Research Team. (2012). A brief assessment of learning for orphaned and abandoned children in low- and middle-income countries. *AIDS and Behavior,* 16(2):480-90. PMCID: PMC3817622. doi: 10.1007/s10461-011-9940-z.

Whetten, K.; Ostermann, J.; Whetten, R. A.; O'Donnell, K.; Thielman, N. T. The Positive Outcomes for Orphans (POFO) Research Team. (2011). More than the loss of a parent: A Multi-Country Study of Orphaned and Abandoned Children. *Journal of Traumatic Stress,* 2011 April; 24(2):174-82. PMCID: PMC3610328. doi: 10.1002/jts.20625.

Whetten, R.; Messer, L.; Ostermann, J.; Whetten, K.; Pence, B. W.; Buckner, M.; Thielman, N.; O'Donnell, K. The Positive Outcomes for Orphans (POFO) Research Team. (2011). Child work and labor among orphaned and abandoned children in five low- and middle-income countries. *BMC International Health and Human Rights,* 2011 January 13; 11:1. PMCID: PMC3037885. doi: 10.1186/1472-698X-11-1.

Messer, L. C.; Pence, B. W.; Whetten, K.; Whetten, R.; Thielman, N.; O'Donnell, K.; Ostermann, J. (2010). Prevalence and predictors of HIV-related stigma among institutional and community-based caregivers of orphans and vulnerable children living in five less wealthy countries. *BMC Public Health,* 2010 August 19;10:504. PMCID: PMC2936424. doi: 10.1186/1471-2458-10-504.

Whetten, K.; Ostermann, J.; Whetten, R. A.; Pence, B. W.; O'Donnell, K.; Messer, L. C.; Thielman, N. M. The Positive Outcomes for Orphans (POFO) Research Team. (2009). A comparison of the well-being of orphans and abandoned children ages six to twelve in institutional and community-based care settings in five less wealthy nations. *PLoS One,* 2009 December 18;4(12):e8169. PMCID: PMC2790618. doi: 10.1371/journal.pone.0008169.

Chapter 3.2

Not only can secure attachment models internalize a solid sense of self as we grow from infancy into toddlerhood, but as we grow, secure attachments in early childhood can help propel us into adolescent stages with a state of mind that is filled with integration, enabling us to become strong and well-developed.

—Dr. Dan Siegel

Reforming Institutions for Young Children in Russian Federation
By Dr. Oleg Palmov,[61] St. Petersburg State University

Institutions in Russian Federation for children zero to four years of age are called baby homes (BHs). Children come to BHs because of parental financial inability to care for a child, the inability of the parents to behaviorally care for the child (e.g., because of parental drug and alcohol abuse, mental health problems, and other mental and behavioral incompetencies), parental unwillingness to rear a child with frank disabilities, and involuntary loss of parental rights because of abuse or neglect (St. Petersburg–USA Orphanage Research Team, 2005).

Children sometimes are temporarily placed into BHs if parents want to take care of the child after solving some of these problems (Muhamedrahimov et al., 2014). Until recently, baby homes were characterized by socio-emotionally depriving conditions in which caregivers direct most of the interactions with children and display a very low level of sensitivity and responsiveness. Children have no opportunity to form close relationships with staff because caregivers care for 12 to 14 children at one time and because children periodically transfer to new groups with different caregivers and peers.

Children potentially experience 60 to 100 different caregivers by two years of age (Muhamedrahimov, 2000; St. Petersburg–USA Orphanage Research Team, 2008).

---

61   See CONTRIBUTORS page for Dr. Palmov's biography.

St. Petersburg, Russian Federation – USA Joint Project in Orphanages: Research-Based Interventions to Promote the Development of Child-Caregiver Relationships

The intervention program developed in this project, and the results of its implementation became the basis for reforming baby homes in the direction of ensuring and protecting the rights of institutionalized children.

The first intervention study, "The Effects of Improving Caregiving on Early Mental Health," conducted in 2000–2005 in St. Petersburg, was designed to promote the development of warm, caring, and socially responsive interactions and attachment relationships between children and caregivers.

Two types of interventions were planned for the orphanages. The first intervention was the training and supervision of the staff aimed at improving the quality of the social environment, especially to promote responsive caregiving. The second intervention was aimed at changing the orphanage's structure and employment patterns, especially to increase the stability and consistency of a few caregivers for each individual child, and to provide an environment that would encourage relationship building.

The overarching purpose of the interventions was to promote the development of warm, caring and responsive social interaction of children with stable and available primary caregivers. Both the training and structural change interventions were provided to one orphanage, only the training to a second, and neither to a third (at any one time Ns = 80-120 in each condition).

The Training Intervention

The training intervention, which is packaged and relatively exportable to other programs and other contexts, focused on teaching caregivers to be socially responsive to children in a warm, caring, respectful, and reciprocal manner.

The train-the-trainers approach was used. Training included all aspects of group care that would support social responsiveness to children (e.g., child development, working with children with disabilities, adult learning styles, team building, supervision, etc.). Infant mental health issues were a special part of the training program with the emphasis on caregiver-infant interaction, attachment, emotional availability of caregivers, and coping with grief and loss in young children.

The Structural Changes Intervention

A set of structural changes was aimed at improving the stability and consistency of caregivers and providing a family environment for each child that would support relationship building. This set of structural changes consists of the following components.

1. *Group size was cut.* The number of children in the group was decreased from 12 - 13 to 6 – 7.

2. *Each subgroup has their own living/dining room.* To provide the consistency of living space that is family-like and to encourage each subgroup of 6 – 7 children to remain in their own living space to maximize contact with their caregivers, the wards were physically reorganized. Prior to the intervention, the group of 12 to 13 children were housed in wards consisting of a single sleeping room, an eating room that was also used by staff to keep records and occasionally for some play by the children, a living/play room, a toilet/bathroom, and a small kitchen area where food, initially prepared in a single institutional kitchen, was dished up and distributed to the children. After the structural change intervention, both of the two subgroups of 6 – 7 children continued to sleep in one room; but the two other rooms were reassigned one to each subgroup, and the assigned room was to serve as dining/living/play room only for that subgroup. To implement this change, some of these two rooms had to be made physically separate by sliding doors.

3. *Graduations were stopped.* The practice of "graduating" children periodically to new caregivers was stopped, which

cut the number of different caregivers a child would see by 60 – 80%.

4. *Children were integrated by age and disability status.* Newly arriving children were distributed among all the subgroups that had a vacancy. Since new arrivals tended to be young and were mixed with respect to their disability status, assigning new arrivals to whichever subgroup had a vacancy meant that the groups would eventually become integrated with respect to disability status and age.

5. *Primary caregivers were instituted.* To stabilize the staff, each subgroup of 6 - 7 children was assigned two "primary caregivers" (plus a third who substituted). Four other "secondary caregivers" were assigned to the group. The number of caregivers working on the ward during a week decreased 33% from 9 to 6.

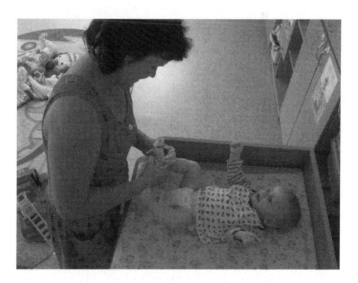

6. *The number of work days for primary caregivers was increased.* To increase the number of times a child sees the primary caregivers during a week, the schedule of their work was changed. Instead of having caregivers who became primary work two to three days (25 hours) a week, they were asked to work five days (forty hours) a week (four days

of seven-hour shifts from 7:30 a.m. to 2:30 p.m. and from 1:30 p.m. to 8:30 p.m. and one day of twelve hours). As a result, children see either or both primary caregivers each day of the week. The secondary caregivers' schedule has not been changed, so they work twenty-four-hour shifts, one in every four days, approximately thirty-six hours per week. If necessary, caregivers get substituted mainly by primary and secondary caregivers for the same subgroup of children.

7. *Family hour was instituted.* To concentrate children's interactions with fewer caregivers, especially with primary caregivers in each subgroup, "family hour" was implemented. Family hour is conducted twice a day, one hour in the morning and one hour in the afternoon. During family hour, the doors between the two living/play rooms of the two subgroups are closed and children and staff are expected to stay in their own subgroup room, presumably playing and in peer or caregiver-child interaction. Primary caregivers remain in the subgroup rooms during family hour, but secondary caregivers, being assigned to the group and not the subgroups, float between the two rooms. Visitors, including the orphanage administration and specialized professionals, are not permitted during family hour. This system of frequent short-term "confinements" to the room of one's subgroup was manageable and enforceable and seemed to accomplish the purpose of setting aside time specifically during which primary caregivers were to interact only with the children in their subgroup.

8. *Pull-out services were changed.* Specialized services, such as massage and some special education activities, were encouraged to be held in the subgroup to the extent possible and appropriate, rather than to pull the child out of the group to a private office as it was before structural changes. Further, to expand the children's experience with age-mates, some activities for children of similar ages and developmental levels from different groups and subgroups were organized

outside of the wards (such as music, swimming, outdoor, and education activities).

9. *Staff teamwork was established.* Staff needed to work in a more team-like fashion than they did before the interventions. Therefore, two teams were organized, each covering half the groups in the baby home. Each team included special teachers, a doctor, and a massage therapist, who observe and analyze the situation in groups and subgroups and plan together with primary and secondary caregivers the organization of daily activities, the development and implementation of the early intervention program for each individual child, staff supervision, and staff interaction. In addition, members of the two teams plus the baby home administrative supervisors constituted the "experts team," and its task is to determine the orphanage general work organization and strategic planning.

The results of this longitudinal study showed that the caregivers in T+SC BH (training plus structural changes baby home no. 13 in St. Petersburg) improved their interactions with children on the wards, and T+SC children increased in physical growth (i.e., height, weight, and head circumference), social-emotional development and attachment to caregivers, and general behavioral/mental development relative to training only (TO) and no intervention (NoI) children. For example, T+SC children's average Battelle Developmental Inventory Developmental Quotients rose from 57 to 92, and improvements increased the longer children were in the T+SC intervention (McCall et al., 2013). So these interventions produced substantial differences in the nature and extent of caregiver-child interactions as well as children's development (The St. Petersburg-USA Orphanage Research Team, 2008).

The intervention and its benefits for children have been maintained after the intervention project ended. There were several components to promote maintenance in original intervention. After funds were terminated, the number of caregivers and caregiver hours available in the T+SC BH (training plus structural changes baby home no. 13

in St. Petersburg) did not change much. A train-the-trainer strategy was adopted. A brief training course was given during and after the intervention period by those specialists originally trained as "trainers." So the staff-training course was continually available to prepare new caregivers. An in-house monitoring and supervision system was established in which specialists (e.g., staff professionals in children with disabilities, early education) were responsible for monitoring the caregivers and encouraging them to implement the training on the wards on a continuing basis.

Additional coaching and technical assistance were provided by two outside professionals that consisted of weekly or bimonthly visitations, supervision, and assistance in periodic refresher training. The second study was conducted to assess development of the children, caregiver-child interactions. It demonstrates that a comprehensive intervention in a St. Petersburg BH was maintained and continued to be associated with better developmental scores for children through the intervention project period as well as for approximately six years after the intervention project ended compared to two comparison BHs. (McCall et al., 2013)

From Research to Changing Policy to Ensure the Rights of Children in Institutions

The research-based intervention program was widely disseminated in baby homes in different regions of Russian Federation. As a result of collaboration between St. Petersburg State University Faculty of Psychology, NGOs, the Public Chamber of the Russian Federation, new research-based requirements of family-oriented social environment for children were included in the resolution on institutions for children in RF (Resolution of the Government of the RF. № 481, 2014). By September 2015, the children's right to develop an individual, personal relationship with the adults who take care of them and know them well had to be implemented through concrete steps listed in the Resolution № 481 in all types of institutions for children zero to eighteen years of age, including those for children with disabilities. The requirements mirror the main components of structural changes (St. Petersburg–USA Orphanage Research Team, 2008): decreasing the number of children in the ward, no transitions between wards, caregiver assignment to the ward, defining the role of primary caregivers, integrating children by age and disability status (basically for BH). Hard process of changing old medically oriented attitudes revealed a high relevance of training and supervision for professionals and caregivers as necessary support for implementing new values.

Further improvement of caregiving through baby homes' staff training and supervision, with the Pikler approach as a source of best practices

The Pikler approach and Lózcy experience reflected in publications, videos, training courses in Emmi Pikler Institute (Budapest, Hungary) provides us with a concrete mechanism to ensure the rights of institutionalized children to be treated as individuals, to experience the acceptance and respect, predictable organization of events in their everyday lives, to satisfy their natural need for activity, to have the possibility of moving and playing freely, to be able to create a positive image of themselves (Rights 2, 3, 4, 5, 6, 7, *Declaration of the Rights of Children in Children's Homes*).

Developed by Emmi Pikler and her colleagues' definitions of respect for the child and cooperation with the child, certain adult behaviors and gestures that provide child experience of trust and respect by the caregiver (Tardos, 2007), have become the necessary additions to the original model of caregiver training in the project "The Effects of Improving Caregiving on Early Mental Health." Two new training modules for the baby home caregivers were developed based on Pikler approach: "Principles of Care with Respect" and "Cooperation with the Child: The Algorithms of Care Procedures." These modules consist of mini lectures, discussions, observations, and exercises and were included as two out of five basic modules for baby homes staff in St. Petersburg, Krasnoyarsk, Novosibirsk (2006–2011), and more than fifty baby homes all over Russian Federation (2012–2016), through the training courses and seminars organized by St. Petersburg State University, Department of Psychology, with participation and financial support of Children's Charity Foundation "Sun City" (Novosibirsk), Regional Public Movement "Petersburg Parents" (St. Petersburg). Followed by supervision, most caregivers show high motivation to use new "Pikler Modules" skills while interacting with children during the daily routines. The new culture of close relationships, respect, and cooperation with the child, as well as ensuring other needs and rights of the children, has become a feature of highly professional attitudes in baby home no. 13 (St. Petersburg), baby home no. 2 (Novosibirsk), baby home no. 3 (Krasnoyarsk), baby homes in Kuybyshev (Novosibirsk region), Usolye Sibirskoe (Irkutsk region), and many others.

References

McCall, R. B.; Groark, C. J.; Fish, L.; Muhamedrahimov, R. J.; Palmov, O. I., and Nikiforova, N. V. (2013). Maintaining a social-emotional intervention and its benefits for institutionalized children. *Child Development, 84,* 1734–1749. http://dx.doi.org/10.1111/cdev.12098.

Muhamedrahimov et al. Behavior problems in children transferred from a socioemotionally depriving institution to St. Petersburg (Russian Federation) families. *Infant Mental Health Journal,* vol. 35(2), 111–112., 2014.

St. Petersburg-USA Orphanage Research Team. (2005). *Characteristics of children, caregivers, and orphanages for young children in St. Petersburg, Russian Federation. Journal of Applied Developmental Psychology*: Child Abandonment, 26, 477–506.

The St. Petersburg-USA Orphanage Research Team. *The effects of early social emotional and relationship experience on the development of young orphanage children* // with commentary by Crockenberg, S.; Rutter, M. Monographs of the society for research in child development, 2008, serial number 291, vol. 73, no. 3

Tardos, A. (Ed.) Bringing up and providing care for infants and toddlers in an institution. – Budapest, 2007 – 211 p.

Chapter 3.3

The unknown energy that can help humanity is that which lies hidden in the child. We must therefore turn to the child as the key to the fate of our future life.

—*Maria Montessori*

Global Family Village, Nepal

Partnering with Communities for Sustainable, Inclusive Care of Orphaned and Abandoned Children in Nepal

By Amy Gedal Douglass, Joy Amulya, Freema Davis, Kishor Shrestha[62]

Introduction

In Nepal, it is estimated that over one million children are orphaned, having lost one or both of their parents,[1] and thousands more are abandoned. These numbers are on the rise, largely resulting from a decade of conflict, political turmoil, and natural disaster that has left many children and families displaced and in extreme poverty.[2,3,4] Although it is well established that traditional institutional rearing has negative effects on children's short-term and long-term development, there arc limited options for orphaned/abandoned children in Nepal who are without family members to care for them.[5,6] Approximately twelve thousand orphaned/abandoned children in Nepal grow up in institutionalized care, which is comprised of traditional orphanages, but predominated by smaller children's homes.

The orphan care system in Nepal, like in many countries, faces many barriers to providing high quality, sustainable care for orphaned/abandoned children. In recent years, there has been a shift to smaller scale children's homes, largely because they are believed to offer higher quality care than large institutions; however, studies have found these homes do not result in better outcomes

---

62 See CONTRIBUTORS page for their biography.

for children than traditional orphanages.[5,7] Research has shown that the majority of children's homes in Nepal struggle to meet even minimum standards of care for children and have high turnover rates because of insufficient and unreliable funding streams from philanthropic organizations and individual donors.[4] Furthermore, in these homes, similar to what is seen in large institutions, children have minimal involvement with the local community as part of their social upbringing, face isolation and marginalization, and fail to develop life skills gained through daily living in a family and village. This makes it difficult for orphaned/abandoned children to integrate into society when they age out of "homes" or orphanages.[5,6]

There is an urgent need for a new model of orphan care that offers a financially sustainable solution for addressing the short and long-term developmental needs of orphaned/abandoned children so that they grow up to become well-adjusted, fully integrated members of society. In response to this issue, Global Family Village (GFV) has created a model of sustainable, inclusive childcare for orphaned/abandoned children, which allows orphans to grow up as fully participating members of village society in a community that is strengthened by the existence of the program for orphaned/abandoned children.

The Global Family Village Model

The GFV model addresses the individual needs of orphaned/abandoned children by partnering with a local community dedicated to a long-term solution for orphaned/abandoned children in their community. Orphaned/abandoned children grow up in a *family house* in a village, where they participated in daily life of family and the community. In addition, the model offers resources to the community, such as an early childhood development (ECD) program and income-generation activities (IGAs) that benefit and strengthen the community as a whole. To make the program sustainable, GFV partners with the local community to adapt the model to meet their community's needs and implement it. Over the course of five to seven years, the community built the capacity with the support of GFV to incrementally take over the financial and operational management of all components of the model, allowing the community to maintain the program in the long run.

The GFV model is comprised of the following five program components:

1. *Transformation of an institutionalized orphanage into a family house* composed of five to eight orphaned/abandoned children and a caregiver "Mother" raised in a family-like environment.
2. *Creation or enhancement of an early childhood development (ECD) program* attended by community children, including those growing up in the family home.
3. *Implementation of income-generation activities (IGAs)* run by community members to raise funds to sustain the program and create economic opportunities for local families.
4. *Development of structured activities to promote interactions between orphaned/abandoned children and the community,* such as a foster grandparent program.
5. *Implementation of community-specific activities that address local needs,* such as providing training to teachers in local schools, making renovations and repairs of the school's physical facilities, promoting local culture and preserving local cultural heritage.

While some program activities contribute directly to promoting the outcomes of orphaned/abandoned children, others create the glue necessary for program success and long-term sustainability by garnering support from the local community for the model and creating reliable funding streams. More specifically, the program is designed to increase knowledge of child development among local families through the ECD program, provide economic opportunities for community members through the IGAs, and offer additional benefits to the community through other program activities. As a result, it is expected that local families will be better positioned to provide for their own families and be more likely to support the GFV model in their community.

Program Objectives

The core objectives of the GFV program include:

- Orphaned/abandoned children grow up in safe and loving environment with access to high quality care and services.
- Orphaned/abandoned children become integrated members of a family and community.
- The local community is strengthened through income-generation activities, capacity building opportunities, and an ECD program for children.
- The local community gains a sense of responsibility and commitment for the orphans and feels ownership of the GFV program.
- The community takes on full financial and management responsibility for the continuation of all program components including the family home within five to seven years.

Findings/Observations

The GFV model has been successfully implemented in Bungamati Village, Nepal, where the program is in its fifth year. The major achievements include the transformation of the orphanage into a family house, the establishment of a thriving ECD program, attended by over 113 community children and growing each year, the development of income-generation activities including a home-stay program, allowing the community to fund 80% of the annual GFV program costs. Further, the children in the family home are growing up as a family, are healthy and well adjusted, succeeding in school, and enjoy friendships and participating in activities in their community. Much progress has been made to develop the capacity of the local partner and develop an infrastructure to assure the maintenance of high quality program components over the long run. However, what really makes this program successful is the buy-in that is growing as a result of the partnership between the local community and GFV. Below is more detail highlighting the accomplishments of each program activity.

Transforming an Orphanage into a Family

The community transformed an existing children's home into a family-like environment. As a "family," they engage in the typical daily life of any other family living in a community. They participate in village activities and festivals, as full-fledged members of the community, resulting in a sense of identity, with a network of friendships once unimaginable. The children attend local schools and receive nutritional, health, and mental health services and are raised in a safe and nurturing environment. The family house is funded, in part, by income generated through the other program components. The local partner, Cooperative Society of Bungamati, has recently started to construct a separate building for the family house with the funds saved from its various income-generating activities, and other donors, including support from GFV. This new home will reduce overhead (currently there are rental fees) and will make the family home a permanent fixture in their community.

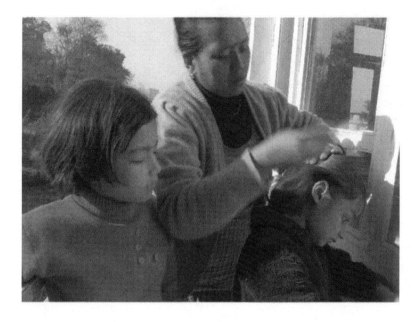

House mother taking care of children in the family house. Photo by Karen Ande.

Establishing an ECD Program in the Community

The local community, with technical assistance from GFV, developed an ECD program that is attended by community children, including those from the family home. The ECD program promotes the development of children and provides opportunities for inclusion of orphaned/abandoned children starting at a young age. Local teachers are trained in developmentally appropriate practices and parents are encouraged to participate and be decision-makers in their children's education. This program component also generates income, through school fees, and creates buy-in for the GFV program by offering valued services that would otherwise not exist in the community. The ECD program was handed over to a local partner, Tri-Ratna Cooperative Secondary School, in the third year of the project period while GFV continued providing technical support. The number of children enrolled in the ECD program has increased to 113 in the 2016 from merely eight in the 2012, the first year of the project.

Children in ECD classroom. Photo by Freema Davis.

Implementing Income-Generating Activities (IGAs)

Local families are provided opportunities to work with community leaders to identify and implement IGAs that build on the community's strengths and resources. For example, in Bungamati Village, which has well-known tourist attractions but lacks a tourism infrastructure, the community has established a home-stay program and plans to open a café. A portion of the income generated through these activities goes to family home, but just as importantly, a portion also goes directly to participating families, creating economic opportunities and strengthening the economic well-being of the community as a whole. The massive earthquake that hit Nepal in April 2015 led to significant setbacks in the income-generation activities of the project. The houses that the villagers updated to welcome tourists for home-stays were seriously damaged, leading to a significant decrease in the number of home stay tourists/visitors. Currently, most of the community financial support for the family home comes from school fees, donations, and home-stay program income from school's guesthouse, though there are plans to revive the home-stay program in the houses after their renovation and reconstruction in the near future.

Creating Structured Activities to Promote the Inclusion of Orphaned/Abandoned Children

The community identified and created the foster grandparent program to promote a sense of community belonging for orphaned/ abandoned children as well as facilitate a sense of responsibility for the children among community members. In this program, children from the family home are matched with local elders, who through a traditional commitment ceremony express their love for the children, share their cultural heritage and take on a sense of obligation for the children. This program has proven to be highly successful. The bonds between the children in the family house and local grandparents were particularly evidence after the 2015 earthquake. Although the lives of the grandparents were severely affected by the earthquake, they remained concerned about the children in the family home. Similarly, the children found ways to comfort and care for the grandparents in the days and weeks following the earthquake.

Children living in the family house with local elderly women bounded as grandparents. Photo by Freema Davis.

Identifying Community-Specific Activities Addressing Local Needs

The local community identified a need for agricultural education programs, teacher-training programs, and renovations of their local secondary school. Together, GFV and the local partner identified resources for implementing these activities. This program component creates buy-in for GFV by demonstrating GFV's commitment to the community.

Conclusion: The Road Forward

GFV is dedicated to improving the lives and outcomes of orphaned/abandoned children. Global Family Village (GFV) envisions a world where every child grows up being an integral part of a supportive family and community. The achievements made so far in piloting this model in Bungamati Village have been encouraging. At the core of the success is the strong belief that this model has the power to transform the way orphaned/abandoned children are cared for and create lasting, systemic change in the childcare system for these children. This model provides an opportunity for sustainable development, builds social cohesion within communities, supports ECD for all, and promotes inclusion of marginalized populations. Further, this model offers a viable alternative to institutionalized non-parental-group residential care for orphaned/abandoned children with family-based community-integrated care. GFV is currently coordinating with the Central Child Welfare Board and other governmental and nongovernmental organizations to expanding this model into other areas in Nepal. While this model has only been piloted in Nepal, given its promise, GFV believes that this model should be tested and replicated in other countries in order to reach the most children in need.

References

1. Central Bureau of Statistics. 2014. Nepal Multiple Indicator Cluster Survey 2014, Key Findings. Kathmandu, Nepal: Central Bureau of Statistics and UNICEF Nepal.

2. UNICEF. "Nepal Statistics Website" Available from: http://www.unicef.org/infobycountry/nepal_nepal_statistics.html

3. ICF Macro, Ministry of Health and Population (Nepal), New ERA. Nepal Demographic and Health Survey 2011. Calverton, United States: ICF Macro.

4. New ERA. Study of Children in Children's Homes in Nepal. Volume I: Main Text. USAID/Nepal. Kathmandu, Nepal. June 2005.

5. Biemba et al. "The Scale, Scope, and Impact of Alternative Care for OVC in Developing Countries." *Critical Review Paper.* Boston University OVC-CARE Project. USAID. Boston, Massachusetts. January 2010.

6. Dozier, M. et al. Institutional Care for Young Children: Review of Literature and Policy Implications. Social Issues and Policy Review 6.1 (2012): 1-25.

7. Abebe, T. "Orphanhood, Poverty, and the Care Dilemma: Review of Global Policy Trends." Social Work & Society, 2009: 7(1), 70-85.

Chapter 3.4

Childhood is not a race to see how quickly a child can read, write and count. It's a small window of time to learn and develop at the pace that is right for each individual child. Earlier is not better.

—Magda Gerber

Casa Ami in Ecuador
A Note from Elsa:

In 2014, my son and I had the privilege of being invited to the home of Maria del Carmen Vásquez and Etienne Moine, who own and run La Casa de los Niños, also known as Casa Ami in Cotacachi, Ecuador. We were welcomed with the loving familiarity one may experience when visiting one's own parents after a long absence away from home.

Photo by Etienne Moine, Casa Ami, Ecuador

My son Leonardo was invited to walk the premises and surroundings and observe activities from a distance during our stay, without interfering in any way, of course. On our last night at Casa Ami, after eating a delicious homemade supper prepared from the vegetable garden, he said, *"Mama, if I hadn't had you as my mother, this is where I would have liked to have grown up."*

He knew this was an orphanage, yet he managed to discern that love was present in every corner and in every living being.

Photo by Etienne Moine, Casa Ami, Ecuador

• • • • • • • • ● ● • • • • • • • •

When I was working with Maria for her contribution to this book, she expressed the need to add another right: "All children have the Right to unconditional love." Because this is the message that she wants to convey to her young residents, she added, "The first three years of life are decisive."

A Brief History of Casa Ami: From an Interview with Co-Founder, María Vásquez

Opened in January 2004, Casa Ami, located 25 kilometers east of Quito, the capital city of Ecuador, is home to 11 children and their three caregivers. Vásquez, who is Ecuadorian, and her French husband, Moine, have owned the property, an organic farm, for 20 years. When the private school where Vásquez had taught closed its doors, she and Moine, who was an administrator at the school, created a home at their farm for children zero to four years old who were living in situations of extreme vulnerability.

They used their own resources to build a beautiful two-story home of wood and natural materials, with Vásquez working tirelessly for two years with government agencies in Ecuador to legally create a foundation, known as AMI, Amigos de la Vida (Friends of Life), a nonprofit organization that oversees Casa Ami.

AMI is also part of a network of diverse institutions of the Metropolitan District of Quito that contributes to creating conditions of respect during the processes of human development. Emphasis is placed on the child's own ability to build himself up, as well as the adult's ability to change that child's attitude, at the same time offering children an opportunity to form a solid foundation that will serve them for the rest of their lives.

It is within this network that Vásquez and Moine have shaped the unique qualities that are Casa Ami, while at the same time, the couple has been able to influence policies that affect the lives of young children in Ecuador. Together with the Metropolitan District of Quito, Vásquez and Moine have also organized international conferences.

What a visitor finds at Casa Ami is a conscientiously thought-out residential nursery where weekly sessions are also held for families with young children that come from the poorest living conditions. Casa Ami also offers a calm and secure environment where children are respected, accepted, and loved.

Casa Ami is not a charity or a methodology but a way of life whose work is guided by the following principles:

- To care without judgment, punishment, or pressure.
- To favorably support children's emotional and physical needs.
- To maintain a prepared and relaxed nurturing environment where children can thrive in all aspects of their health and development and live with joy.

Photo by Etienne Moine, Casa Ami, Ecuador

Casa Ami begins with daily routines that are organized in the following manner:

- After waking up, mornings consist of bathing, breakfast, autonomous play periods, and a snack.
- Afternoons consist of play activities.
- Evenings are time for dinner, preparing for bedtime, and sleep.

It is through these organized events that the team of caregivers conducts its work through language, by setting limits, resolving conflicts, creating anticipation, and instilling feelings of emotional security in the children.

Vásquez also encourages children to have personal belongings, as is suggested in this book's second Right. She also makes sure that children learn to differentiate what is *theirs* from what belongs to others.

At the same time, Vásquez's team of caregivers has been instructed to let the child know, as he watches attentively, that she is taking out his clothes from his shelf. As he begins to internalize that he does, in fact, have his own shelf, his own clothes, and even his own crib, he develops a consciousness of what and where his belongings are. This helps develops a healthy separation of himself from others.

When morning comes, through the caregiver's signals with her actions and voice, the children anticipate what will be happening. For example, it is Xavier's turn to have his diaper changed. Through the repetition of these actions, and being included in the process, the child comes to know the routine and understands that social cues will serve him in the future.

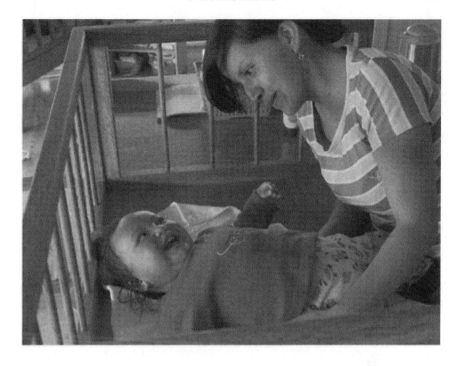

Photo by Etienne Moine, Casa Ami, Ecuador

Yes, the child will learn to have to wait his turn, but this, in essence, is the basis for garnering respect.

After dinner, the child is offered simple choices, such as being asked by his caregiver which pajamas he would like to wear. *"The red ones or the blue ones?"* By having the opportunity to assert himself, he is building qualities that will later lead him to a more confident path of self-expression.

Photo by Etienne Moine, Casa Ami, Ecuador

Vásquez explained that the caregivers are emotionally supported and that the environment is auto-therapeutic (self-therapy) or one "not needing actual psychotherapy for the caregivers." *"I am in constant communication with the caregivers in various ways. By observing them during their daily caregiving routines I am able to better understand each situation.*

"I meet with them individually as many times as needed," she continued, *"in addition to our weekly and monthly group meetings. Through self-reflection, we converse about the importance of quality care toward the children in a peaceful and relaxed environment that meets the children's sensory motor stages of development. I make it a point to let caregivers know that I am always available for them."*

Because Casa Ami offers an environment of respect, when the caregivers are faced with internal processes of personal difficulties, Vásquez might say, *"Lupe, I am under the impression that you raised your voice when interacting with Armando. I see the work that you do here, and notice in you a great sensitivity when connecting with children. How are you feeling? I see that you have difficulty in setting boundaries, but that is no reason for reacting to the child."*

Vásquez's support to the caregivers in these situations is humane and kind, and she never abandons them in times of difficulty. Limits correspond not only to children, but also to the caregivers, and they involve gentle reminders of respectful awareness.

"Limits are important for building one's identity," said Vásquez. *"Even nature herself imposes limits on us, and adults often have difficulty setting them."*

When stressing the difference between healthy house rules and abandonment, Vásquez added, *"Without boundaries a child may become defiant and chaotic when it comes to applying respect."*

In addition, Vásquez stressed the importance of being close to the child, without punishing or shaming him, but simply establishing a limit with consistency and never making him suffer over it.

In short, the loving and nurturing environment at Casa Ami offers children the possibility of self-regulation.

Photo by Etienne Moine, Casa Ami, Ecuador

There are no mandatory courses in Ecuador that prepare a caregiver to work at Casa Ami, as the type of care that is expected comes from self-reflection and the awareness of absolute respect for the child at all times. It is also important that the caregiver pays close attention to not generate emotional dependencies that would incapacitate or confuse the child when reintegrating to a family life.

Caregivers are never called *Mom, Dad, Auntie,* or *Uncle,* thus offering a distinction when they are adopted or returned to their natural families. Before a new caregiver is allowed to work directly with the children, she begins by only observing, which is then followed by her interacting with inanimate objects, such as the furniture, clothing, and/or toys.

During this process, she is encouraged to narrate her actions, saying, *"I am taking this tray. I am putting away this sweater. I am picking up the toys."*

Afterward, the caregiver is encouraged to do the same, but this time, by narrating the activity before it happens because this is the expected communication toward the children. The caregiver then practices with a doll, and when Vásquez sees that a care provider is confident and fluent in her narrative (generally within a month), she is able to begin interacting one-on-one with the four children that will be under her care.

The caregivers at Casa Ami offer children a safe and nurturing environment where they can enjoy periods of uninterrupted activity that support their unique neurobiological development. Weekly walks around the neighborhood offer children an opportunity to socialize naturally.

Photo by Etienne Moine, Casa Ami, Ecuador

Photo by Etienne Moine, Casa Ami, Ecuador

Because children have the right to know their personal history
and to get support to stay in contact with their families, María adds
that every child welcomed at Casa Ami is given information about
his current personal situation from the moment of their arrival.

It is very important to communicate to the child any news about
his personal history with anticipation. This offers him an opportunity
to prepare emotionally to receiving information that could at times be
painful. Depending on his personal circumstances and the complexity
of certain situations, we convene with him when it doesn't interfere
with his routine.

The child's primary caregiver must attend such meetings. Since
she is the one he trusts, she can provide the nurturing support needed
for his emotional stability.

In advance, the social worker or director of the institution
prepares the conversations to be had with the child. His development
and physical and emotional states are taken into consideration. It

is necessary to use simple, clear and descriptive language, free of judgment. Because a child's logic during early childhood is developing, we avoid verbalizations that have to do with cause and effect.

The child's organism is capable of understanding reality and come to his own conclusions if respected through his life's process. The child is attentive to what the adult has to say. He expresses his feelings through movements, gestures, and sound. He may ask to know the place where he was found, the people that cared for him, or to visit a family member. Our institution is committed to doing whatever it takes to meet the child's wishes.

To speak the truth to the child and inform him about his life and his family are references of respect and dignity as he builds his identity.

The adult's main role is to present herself with clarity and transparency. She lets the child know that she cares for him and that she has a name. She doesn't request to be called any name that belongs within a family nucleus. This way, the child can hold that space for the family that resides within his emotions and cells.

No matter how small the child is, he has innate resources registered in his internal programming that will allow him to face and overcome trauma and experiences that have caused him great suffering. He is able to resume proper direction for his life. But this is only possible if the adults tending to him are attentively caring and nurturingly supportive and offer a calm atmosphere rich in didactic materials, where the child can satisfy his sensory motor needs with out threats, dangers, conditioning, or expectations.

The child needs to exercise his ability to make decisions, follow his own interests, and practice skills with autonomy and spontaneity.

An environment that offers love and respect to the child favors his auto-therapeutic process. This is where the child can express himself as he is, externalize his discomforts, and restructure experiences for the development of a solid and flexible personality. Only through these means can the child contribute positively to his family, be it biological or adoptive, and not be a heavy burden to himself and others.

Aside from being a residential nursery, Casa Ami also offers a day program where children living in family settings, can enjoy all that such a nurturing and magical place has to offer.

Joyce Gallardo[63] also had the privilege of visiting Vásquez and Moine at Casa Ami and writes about that visit here:

My Day at Casa Ami

Every morning at the same time, Maria del Carmen Vásquez and the older children went for a long walk regardless of the weather. As she and I made our way to the house, I saw the three older children run to the gate to greet her. Vásquez greeted each child at his eye level, taking their hands or touching them lightly on the shoulder, speaking softly and clearly as she told them that she had come to take them for their walk.

Photo by Etienne Moine, Casa Ami, Ecuador

---

63   Joyce Gallardo has been an early childhood educator for nearly three decades. See CONTRIBUTORS page for her biography.

I noticed that their speech was limited and that they basically repeated key words from sentences they'd heard Vásquez say before they went off on their walk. The children love this lush organic garden and help the adults harvest and prepare fresh vegetables daily for their meals.

I was struck by the many similarities to Lóczy, not only in the physical environment of Casa Ami, but also in the manner in which the caregivers walked slowly and stooped down to speak to the children on their level. The children also spent much of their time outdoors in the mild climate.

Photo by Etienne Moine, Casa Ami, Ecuador

The house itself featured low wooden tables and stools for playing and for eating, while the children's little wooden beds were handcrafted. The indoor play area was inviting, clean, and well ordered, and the aroma of lunch being cooked wafted through the house, making it feel like a home where people lived and loved.

As I sat watching Galo, who was almost three, trying to put on his shoes, his caregiver encouraged him in a soft voice, but did not offer her help. He managed to put on one shoe, and with a bit of help from the caretaker, he put on his other shoe, before running off to play.

Outside, two children watched the gardener dig and rake the soil. A small bird hopped across the mat where a 10-month old baby lay on his back playing with his hands. Vásquez had told me that this baby had been found in the trash as a newborn.

At this point, his caregiver told him she was going to pick him up, taking him tenderly in her arms and putting a bib on him. She offered him food from a glass to drink, giving him her undivided attention, and when he was finished drinking, she put him down in his crib, announcing first what she was going to do.

Another caretaker called the children inside to fetch their bibs and bring them to her to tie, after which each child was given freshly-made pineapple juice in a plastic pitcher to carry outside to drink. The children sat down at a table on stools they had carried out, and poured their own juice. One little girl sat by herself, as she was not yet ready to join the other children, the caretaker sitting nearby.

A peaceful, calm environment such as this, with predictability, consistency, and continuity, had not been a part of these children's young lives before coming to Casa Ami. I was informed that when the children arrived at Casa Ami, they manifested signs of aggression, boredom, hyperactivity, lack of concentration, and other mental and physical difficulties as a result of the often stressful and unprotected environments into which they had been born.

Photo Etienne Moine, Casa Ami, Ecuador

This lack of protection and the lack of physical and psychological nourishment, had profoundly affected these children. But at Casa Ami, they came to rely on the rhythm of each day to always be the same, where an orderly hum of activity helped to heal them.

When I left Casa Ami, the sun was high in the sky and the fields and gardens seemed to glisten. I waved good-bye, saying, 'Adios, niños. Adios.'

Photo Etienne Moine, Casa Ami, Ecuador

Back home in North America, I remained inspired in my work with the young children in my care. What I saw at Casa Ami—the courage, sacrifice, dedication, and spirit of generosity—continues to resonate with me.

Photo by Etienne Moine, Casa Ami, Ecuador

Chapter 3.5

Peace really begins with us. The peace in the adult is conveyed to the baby through words, looks, hands, and attitude. We can't pretend to feel peaceful when we don't feel peaceful. So we have to work on ourselves if we are to bring peace to babies. Gandhi once said, 'We must be the change we wish to see in the world.' I rephrased Gandhi's saying as 'We must be the change we wish to see in the world.'

—*Janet Gonzalez-Mena*

A Professor's Journey
By Denise Da Ros-Voseles, PhD[64]

Caregivers play such an important role when caring for our young ones. They are not only giving the care, but they are also receiving a great gift from each child during every interaction together. Denise Da Ros-Voseles started out as a van driver at an orphanage and went on to care for the infants and toddlers there. She is currently a professor at Northeastern State University in Tahlequah, Oklahoma, and recognizes the gift that her work at an orphanage gave her.

Growing up in the 1970s, my early experiences influenced my philosophy of care, with my first foray into caring for children in a group setting in Rockton, Illinois. At that time, the program's focus was crisis intervention for abused and neglected children, infants to 13 years.

I was placed in the infant and toddler room to meet the physical and emotional needs of these very young children—changing diapers, dressing them, and occasionally taking them on outings off campus. Because of this experience, I was hired as the part-time van driver at Oak Grove Children's Home in North Charleston, South Carolina.

Oak Grove began as Charleston Orphan House, established in 1790, making it the oldest municipal orphanage in the United States.

---

64 Denise Da Ros-Voseles, PhD, is a professor and chair of the early childhood program at Northeastern State University. See CONTRIBUTORS page for her biography.

From van driver, I was promoted to activities director and eventually to assistant to the director. The campus had large grassy areas, cottages, an administration building with sleeping quarters, and an elementary school within walking distance.

House parents, with degrees in sociology and psychology, lived in the cottages, and there were also two relief house parents who covered during days off. Each cottage had a cook/housekeeper who, to me, were the heart and soul of the cottages, providing meals, good counsel, and both approval and disapproval.

There was other support staff as well, including two social workers and the director, with a psychiatrist available for consultations.

Children living there were referrals from social services, court-ordered placements, or families requesting that their children temporarily live at the city-supported facility. The typical cottage housed eight to ten similarly aged children of the same sex, with the house parents firm but nurturing, and who collaborated with the social workers.

I recall the good will within the community, including providing doctor visits at a nearby medical university. And although the director advocated tirelessly for children to be able to lead stable and healthy lives until their parents regained custody, were able to bring their children home, or would age out, I realized that this wasn't always easy.

Nevertheless, I look back on this time with fondness, and as a young adult, being able to care for children directly and indirectly led me to where I am today, which is teaching infant development at the university level.

My students quickly see how important the early years are and the implications they have for older children. Dr. Emmi Pikler is acknowledged for her pioneering contributions in infant-toddler care. As the syllabus states, "Foundational to the care and education of the very young is the role of relationships built on respect."

As we unpack this statement, teacher candidates develop an appreciation of how providing careful personalized attention during daily and necessary caregiving routines leads to trust. Since many of my students are parents and even grandparents, this is an important revelation. Teacher candidates are also invited to contemplate the role hands play as they listen to my reading of an excerpt from Dr. Pikler's book, "Peaceful Babies-Contented Mothers".

On so many levels, the trajectory for growth and development is established in the early years. Students leave the course with a deepened appreciation of the role of respectful caring of infants and toddlers, the children in their future classrooms, and their own children—present and future.

Chapter 3.6

Where there is love, there is life.

—Mahatma Gandhi

My Experience Living at Thompson Orphanage
By Stella Henson[65]

While it is true that some children can't accept institutionalized life, there are those that thrive, as well as feel safe and secure, in those homes. I have talked to many foster children, and most tell me that they felt they never belonged, no matter how nice a foster family was to them. But I also think of all the lives that could have been saved if orphanages offered optimal conditions and were not considered damaging for children.

Before I went to live at Thompson Orphanage, my two sisters and I lived with my mother in her mother's home. My parents had separated when I was six years old, and I never saw my dad again, who died when I was eight.

Mother had to work, and my deaf grandmother looked after my sisters and me, but after mother became critically ill, I was put in Thompson Orphanage in 1945. At first, I hated the orphanage and told that to my brother who had been in the army.

He then told our mother, who wrote me a letter and said, *"Stella, honey, I guess you will always be miserable like me."* Suddenly, I realized that I had a choice as to how to think, and even though I loved mother dearly, I did not want to be unhappy all the time. I straightened up and stopped resenting everything that I was told to do.

I started looking at everything around me, and if a negative thought came, I would replace it with something positive. There will

---

65   Stella Henson has written about her life in an orphanage. Her book, *Memories of Thompson Orphanage*, is testimony to the fact that orphanages can—and do—produce wonderful results.

always be negative things in a person's life, but it's how we deal with them that makes all the difference.

We had responsibilities at the orphanage, and those responsibilities taught me to do things that I had never done. Girls learned how to can and freeze vegetables that the boys grew on our farm. I learned how to do everything, from working in the dining room to working in a laundry. There were just so many things that I was exposed to that would have never happened had I not been brought up in the orphanage.

After I graduated from high school, I was allowed to stay at Thompson until I finished Kings Business College. All the things I learned during those years prepared me for the world on my own. And although several of the boys and girls I grew up with didn't want anyone to know they were in an orphanage, I am proud that I was blessed with such a wonderful life filled with opportunities that I would never have had.

It is sad when a child can't stay with his family, where most of the time he is loved, but it's a blessing that they can go to a place where his every need is the main focus. Teach him pride, and set guidelines for the child, and someday that child will be a credit to himself, family, and country.

Children are the world's future, and let's never forget how important each one is, because one person can change the course of a life for the better. I know because I was a blessed child.

Chapter 3.7

Mutual caring relationships require kindness and patience, tolerance, optimism, joy in the other's achievements, confidence in oneself, and the ability to give without undue thought of gain.

—Mr. [Fred] Rogers

Care Practices for Children in Homes in Uganda

Experiences and opportunities from SOS Children's Village in Uganda

By Ronald Ssentuuwa

According to Prof. Yanghee Lee, *"Millions of children around the world are without, or at risk of losing, parental care. They face significant challenges in their daily lives, which can affect them well into adulthood."* This situation is not different in Uganda where, according to the Orphans and Vulnerable Children report in 2015, 2.43 million children are orphans and 8 million are either critically or moderately vulnerable (NSPPI II 2011/12-2015/16).

In addition, there are approximately 10,000 children living on the streets of Kampala Capital City and other major towns across the country, mostly because of neglect, abuse, and poverty. The situation is worsened by the political and economic situation, and families struggle to meet the social needs of their children. Thus, a quarter of households in Uganda have at least one orphan in an average family size of six members.

In this regard, SOS Children Village in Uganda began work in 1991 in the wake of the terrible destruction wrought by military war in 1986 that left many children abandoned. Our vision is that *every child deserves a family and to grow up with love, respect, and security.*

So far, we directly support close to 9,000 children and young adults and over 30,000 community members indirectly. With four different Children Villages in Uganda—Kakiri and Entebbe in Wakiso District, Fort Portal Kabarole district, and Gulu in Gulu District—we provide care, education, health interventions, capacity-building, and advocacy.

In an effort to promote holistic development of children, music, dance, and drama sessions have been integrated into their routines. Children at the village can now play a coordinated tune on traditional instruments. This has not only kept children busy, but it has also worked in the psycho-social rehabilitation of the children, as well as boosting their esteem.

In December 2014, a total of 693 children (58.4% boys, 46.2% girls) were being cared for in the family-based care program. SOS Uganda has its own kindergarten and continues to offer quality and competitive infant education based on the internally designed curriculum that complies with the government's early childhood development requirements.

SOS Children Village provides medical facilities for curative and preventive health services to children and their caregivers living in the children village, as well as for the local communities. Services provided include: immunization, malaria prevention and treatment, family planning, sexual reproductive health, and community outreach.

Besides the care for children in the family-based program, there are community initiatives that focus on capacity building; household sanitation and hygiene improvement; lowering school drop-out rates; and support to several income-generating activities through *village savings and lending associations.* These interventions help strengthen household economics and protect children against abuse.

SOS Children Village in Uganda has seen children grow as responsible citizens. Beneficiaries of our program have stated that our program provided them with a safe childhood, thus allowing them to develop to their fullest potential. This is manifested with many being employed in various capacities, having completed school with different professional qualifications.

One is now married and said she opted to stay home to take care of her children, just as her caregivers, who are called *mothers,* had taken care of her. She has further been able to mobilize women to have business skills by inviting community role models and speakers who own local businesses, to inspire and motivate the vulnerable women, many of whom started their own businesses.

We also care for abandoned children, and this is the testimony of a *mother* in the SOS children Village who took take of a two-year-old girl who was abandoned in a hospital and was being cared for by a Good Samaritan. *"The little girl was malnourished, weighed less than five kilograms, and could not move. Doctors estimated that she required a seven-month rehabilitation treatment."*

With loving nurturing from the SOS *mother,* coupled with effective care and recommended feeding practices, *"We left the hospital in seven days instead of seven months! Children need care and love, and that was precisely what this little girl needed,"* reported the SOS *mother.*

Unfortunately, there is a growing number of children falling into institutional care across the globe. *Save the Children* notes that millions of children around the world live in child-care institutions (CCIs), where some may lack individual care and a suitable environment to fulfill their potential. Such conditions may impact all aspects of child development: social, emotional, intellectual, and physical attributes, resulting in slower brain development, insecure attachment, and loss of connection with the family and community.

The situations are worsened by CCIs not having a child protection policy. In Uganda, it is estimated that 55% of the CCIs exist illegally, 70% have inadequate child records and 50% have completely unacceptable care standards, where the child-caregiver ratio stands at 1 per 20 children. This is beyond the current family status that stands at 1 to 6 on average, and further limits the early stimulation and interaction with children.

There is a need to ensure concerted efforts to avert such situations, given the population growth in sub-Saharan Africa. A case in point is that Uganda is the second country with the youngest population in the world at fifty one percent (51%), of which over 40,000 children live in CCIs, though it is evident that when given the proper conditions, children grow well with their biological parents, families, and communities.

Photo Credit: Michela Morosini

It is for this reason that Uganda has prioritized alternative care to avert the increasing number of children falling into CCIs. *The Alternative Care Consortium on System Strengthening* is a three-year project that aims to reintegrate children with their families. It considers both the formal and informal alternative care options. By strengthening communities and families to take care of their own children, the goal is to effectively secure children's well-being across the continuum of care.

All photos by SOS Children Village Uganda

Chapter 3.8

When a child can relate what he learns to his own experiences, his vital interest is awakened, his memory is activated, and what he has learned becomes his own.

—Rudolf Steiner, philosopher, author, and educator

The Creation of the Kinder Haus in Berlin, Germany[66]
By Pia Dögl and **Elke-Maria Rischke** [67]

In 2004, nine people founded a nonprofit association to set up round-the-clock care for babies and young children that had been neglected or experienced trauma. The aim was to care for children affected by violence, abuse, or neglect in a family-like situation for a limited period.

In 2005, cofounders Ute Strub (longtime movement and Pikler educationalist), Elke-Maria Rischke (longtime Waldorf educationalist), and Pia Dögl (educationalist and businesswoman) rented an old farmhouse in Brandenburg, Germany, 80 kilometers from Berlin.

In order to ensure a family-like environment, they decided that a maximum of 12 children from 0-6 years old should live in two groups, with each group having a supervising caregiver who lived with the children in the house. She was supported by two other caregivers and trainees working in shifts.

The Concept of the Facility
We wanted to enable therapeutic provisions for babies and small children to be a holistic part of everyday life, thus painting the rooms in calming and harmonious colors. In addition, the play materials were predominantly made of natural materials that would allow the

---

66 In this section, authors talk about the beginnings of The Kinder Haus in Berlin, when professionals were trained in the Pikler approach. That has now changed, and the current staff is no longer trained under this approach.

67 See CONTRIBUTORS page for their biographies.

children a wide range of sensuous experiences, as well as the widest possible scope for the development of their creativity.

It was intended that the house should not seem like an institution, with a large inviting kitchen and a comfortable sofa in each playroom. There was also a large terrace, a spacious garden with a big sandpit, a natural spring for playing with water, a swing, and fruit trees and flowers and herbs, all giving the children additional opportunities for movement, activity, and play.

Various Pikler and Hengstenberg movement materials (www. Spielzeugmacher.at) were set up in the playrooms and on the terrace. Included were a crawling crate with attachable crawling ramps for the smaller children and, in the eating area, eating benches developed by Pikler and playpens that provided protected areas for the children's needs in their respective stages of development.

Caregivers that lived in the house had rooms on the upper floor, which also had sanitary facilities, a large recreation room, an office, and a therapy room.

This quiet rural setting amid nature had a healing effect on the children, as did the sheep, cows, and other animals on the property. Walks were plentiful, with the children enjoying visits to a nearby farm where they could watch the workers or were allowed to help.

Our aim was for the children to find peace and quiet and stabilize themselves emotionally and physically.

Empathy and Respectful Care

An attentive and respectful relationship was fundamental to us in the daily care routines of the babies as well as the older children. It became apparent that even heavily traumatized children began to trust their caregivers after a short time because the children were treated with care: being told what was happening, concurrently given time to get used to the idea, and because they felt that their reactions were being taken seriously.

For example, an eight-week-old girl came to us, having been diagnosed with "serious infant depression." She had experienced no love from her mother, including never having had reciprocal eye contact. As a result, the baby didn't react to being spoken to, nor did she respond to sounds or changes in the light. She also drank very little.

With the empathetic and respectful care approach, changes soon became apparent: The child reacted to being spoken to; she began following her caregiver's moving lips; and she began drinking more.

Several weeks later, when the child psychiatrist who had initially referred her to us, visited, he didn't recognize the baby who was now interested in what was going on around her, as well as reacting to him by giving him a smile.

Independent Motor Development

Most of the children who came to the Kinder Haus, irrespective of age, had limited motor skills or were insecure or overanxious. They obviously had had few opportunities to move around freely, and for most of the older children, playing outdoors was new to them.

When overanxious children found the courage, for example, to jump from a bale of straw into soft hay, they achieved greater mental stability, because they probably had little opportunity to try things out for themselves, learn to judge their limits, or find their balance on uneven ground, all of which ultimately leads to developing a healthy feeling in their bodies.

Individual Playtimes

So that the children could also have an adult to themselves from time to time, there was a two-hour playtime once or twice a week, which took place in a staff member's living room that was partly fitted out as a playroom.

The idea was that the children saw how adults lived, also learning that there are things belonging to adults that can be looked at but are not toys to play with. But it was play that was most important. The children developed imaginative games with relatively few objects, while playtimes also enriched play in groups, with the children appearing more balanced and content.

Participation in Daily Life

The older children enjoyed helping prepare breakfast and supper and were allowed to do so as independently as possible. Emptying the dishwasher or the small sink were much sought-after activities as well.

Being able to do something meaningful also enabled the children to recognize that their lives were meaningful, which is especially important for children growing up in a home.

In addition, the children who wanted to could help hang up the wash, watch work done at the sewing machine, and dig in the garden, where they could plant and water flowers. The neighbors were also well-disposed toward the children and were pleased to see them happy in their wider surroundings.

Celebrations

An important part of the children's lives were seasonal festivals, birthdays, and leaving parties. Visits from musicians, who played works by Mozart, Bach, and Vivaldi, were also happy times, with the children quietly listening or happily dancing. Celebrating Sundays was also a part of all this, where an occasional puppet show would be followed by dancing, singing, or games.

Saying Farewell

When one of the children transferred to a foster family or a caregiver was leaving, there was a "banquet" for everyone in the house, with cake, cocoa, and the giving of flowers as presents.

Each child who left received a diary. It recorded the child's development steps at the Kinder Haus, various events, and also small anecdotes supplemented with photos.

It was important that children who knew nothing about the beginning of their lives or why they came should at least have no holes in their biographies from the time they were at the Kinder Haus.

The Children's Personal Property

We also thought it important that children should be allowed to keep toys that they had brought with them or received as presents over the course of time as their personal property.

The older children each had a little cabinet beside their beds to store and look after their "valuables"; the small children had a cloth bag for their own toys. It was important for children to wear their own clothes when they first arrived, but when they outgrew them, the children enjoyed going "shopping" in the storage cupboard, where what they chose became their own.

Medical and Therapeutic Provision

Regular doctor's visits

Our anthroposophical pediatrician (a Rudolf Steiner-based spiritual philosopher), made regular visits to Kinder Haus to carry out necessary examinations and provide vaccinations. During visits, the doctor spent time with each child, whether or not it was medically necessary, so that a mutually trusting relationship was developed.

Additional treatments included craniosacral therapy, oil dispersion baths, and speech therapy.

Exchange of Information about the Children

Regular discussions regarding each child involved all of the staff and usually included the children's doctor. The aim was to bring together a wide range of observations about the child and, thus, reach a deeper understanding of his needs.

The reviews could be regarded as part of the therapy, and the children discussed in this way were generally more balanced.

Did the Children Feel at Home at the Kinder Haus?

Because babies cannot yet express their feelings in words, we needed to observe them carefully: What is expressed in their overall behavior, gestures, or body tension? Do they open up to their surroundings with joy and interest? Do they show a readiness to relate, or if not, can they become capable of relating to others?

On the other hand, older children could talk about how they felt, and if they were sad or suffered from homesickness, this was usually expressed before going to sleep or at mealtimes.

It goes without saying that all the children would have preferred to have stayed with their parents. However, when they were playing and active, they forgot their homesickness, and it seemed as if they were using every opportunity to be happy. At these times there was no indication that most of them had left a difficult past.

As a result of their similar fates, some children felt strongly connected to one another, like siblings, and stayed in touch years later. It was important that during the time they were with us, the children could feel they were both seen and valued as themselves.

Cooperation with the Parents

In agreement with the Youth Welfare Office, parents, usually mothers, were allowed to visit their child once a week for up to three hours. In individual cases, visits were also possible more often, with some children allowed to spend the weekend at home. When the well-being of the child was at risk, visits were prohibited.

Not all parents took up the offer of visits, and some forgot the appointment or spent the money the Youth Welfare Office had provided for the journey on other things.

It was a difficult situation for the children to bear when an expected visit was cancelled, even more so for those children who never received visits. In those cases, we tried to do something special with these children so that they would also have some news to tell. This could not, however, alleviate their distress, but the children did have the opportunity to express their sadness, to have a good cry, and above all, to feel understood in their sorrow.

Discussions with Parents

Parental visits were followed by individual discussions with the parents. It was important to build a relationship with the parents, to give them space to tell us how they were getting on, what they wanted for their child, and what expectations they had of us.

Whenever contact with the parents was possible and helpful, we aimed to promote and maintain it. In most cases, it was clear that these parents themselves had never or had not received sufficient love and appreciation.

It was also important for the children that we spoke with, and about their parents, with respect and appreciation. Despite everything they had done to their child or not provided them with, we made sure that we dealt respectfully with the parents.

Looking Like a Stranger

It was difficult for parents to see their children in strange new clothes and perhaps also notice that they smelled differently because of a different washing powder or soap. These external changes reinforced their fear that their child could also inwardly become a stranger to them.

In addition, some parents said that they could never offer their child what they were getting at the Kinder Haus, neither in terms of content nor for financial reasons. In our experience, it is helpful to all involved to build up authentic contact by addressing parents' insecurities directly.

The more the parents felt heard and understood, the more they were ready for positive cooperation.

Avoiding Conflicts of Loyalty

In working with parents or other family members, we always were conscious that the children should not slip into a conflict of interest or loyalty. One example concerned a four-year-old boy who returned to the Haus after a weekend visit to his mother and her partner, when he had his head shaved.

His main caregiver was shocked and outraged, as it seemed as if protection had been taken from his head, not to mention his disconcerting appearance. It was important that the boy not experience his caregiver as being critical but that his caregiver stand behind him and love him, no matter what had happened and however he looked.

At a later parent discussion, his mother could be told that her son did not feel good with his new haircut and that the other children spoke to him disparagingly. Together with his mother, we tried to see what her son needed so that he could feel safe and sound.

We learned that it was the mother's partner who wanted the boy to have his head shaved and were then able to discuss what she needed as a mother in order to not let herself be influenced by her partner, thus losing sight of her child's needs.

Staff Selection

It was a great challenge to find qualified staff who were prepared to care for children in a family-like situation, i.e., around the clock and to live with them. In Germany, the law requires that all caregivers are recognized by the state, with management tasks requiring several years of experience.

Personal Attitude and the Preparedness for Self-Education

The caregivers' attitudes and willingness to develop were fundamental preconditions for working with the children, necessitating that the following questions be answered when applying for a job:

- How is the child regarded? Is the child seen as ill or psychologically disturbed?
- Is the child labeled with conventional concepts of illness, such as "hyperactive," "depressive," etc.?
- Is it a question of merely practically attending to the children with feeding and changing diapers, etc., or is there an understanding for how caring situations can proceed empathetically and gently?
- How is bonding built up? Is it a question of bonding the child to them? And how will the child be accompanied to "gain a foothold" in a future living situation?
- Will contact with the child be maintained as far as questions of location and time allow?
- How are one's own childhood experiences reflected?

- To what extent are one's own needs for closeness, love and appreciation, conscious?

Sometimes we found out that caregivers were applying for jobs at the Kinder Haus because they wanted to find a home for themselves. Loneliness and self-esteem issues are unsuitable for this profession as long as they remain unaddressed.

The Staff As the Driving Force

Because it was difficult to find caregivers who were prepared to take responsibility for the children around the clock, we were finally forced to work exclusively in shifts. Unfortunately, this gave the work a stronger institutional feel rather than a more family-like one.

It happened frequently that caregivers did not stay for more than a year because they had imagined the work would be less arduous. Most of them hadn't imagined what it means to look after babies and small children in residential care. They seemed to have the fantasy that everything would be comparable to a kindergarten class. Here, however, the children do not go home in the afternoon.

In short, the frequent turnover of main caregivers was not beneficial for the children.

Maintaining a Relationship With Children After Leaving the Kinder-Haus

Some caregivers from the Kinder Haus are still in contact with the children they formerly cared for, and visit them wherever they might be—in a residential institution or a foster family—or take them on excursions.

The intention is that these children who had been left by their parents should not have to experience being left once again, particularly when the caregiver was the first person with whom the child had developed a relationship. This experience of loyalty enables children to want to bond fully with their foster parents.

The older the children become, the greater the value they place on these contacts. Those who are now 13 and 14 years old are increasingly asking more about their time at the Haus, and they want to find out more about this part of their lives. Some have said to their former main caregivers, *"You were actually our mum (to us) at the Kinder Haus."*

Most of the foster parents also experience contact with former caregivers as supportive and helpful, and some get in touch when difficulty arises.

I believe that unarmed truth and unconditional love will have the final word.

—Martin Luther King, Jr.

Closing Words from Anna Tardos

With this book, we try to help children who are in institutions, in infants' homes, or in children's homes who cannot have or feel the love of a mother or family. They have a right to a happy childhood and to become healthy and happy adults. We wrote primarily about infants and young children, an especially sensitive age range, who need to be taken care of not only with good intentions but also with a special expertise.

Infants' homes still exist in many countries around the world. Many people consider them hopeless situations. Unfortunately, it is true that in many places, the lives of children living there are not worthy of a child's life. For instance, they have to sleep in huge dormitories, often with 50 other children, with constantly rotating or changing adults who often have to take care of 10 to 15 children at the same time. Thus, the care becomes quick and impersonal. These conditions make it impossible for the children to enjoy a genuine childhood, to receive individual treatment, and to have positive experiences. This is why numerous people in many countries want to abolish infants' homes.

What we tried to demonstrate in this book is that closing down all infants' homes is neither realistic nor does it solve the problem. As long as there are children still living in institutions—and there are—our task is to improve their lives, and in many cases, or in many places from around the word, people have applied effort to improve children's lives.

The purpose of our writing was to help understand that our task is not only to ameliorate the situation of children living in children's homes, but our task is far greater; our task is to offer children a joyful and loving childhood.

In order to implement this, it is not enough that we are guided by good intentions. It is not enough that we love children in general. There are numerous conditions to ensure that a young child will receive all he needs in an institutional setting, as well, i.e., living in a group of children, cared for not by a mother but by several caregivers.

This book is only the beginning, and hopefully, the information in this book will help you find renewed applications to your work. It is a mission—and not an easy task—but it can be done. It is also not hopeless to try because it is for the children.

Finally, it is our humble aspiration that the information shared in this book can become a seed for a better upbringing of our most vulnerable children. Perhaps we can have a better world, a better humanity. And this, in turn, might help us on the road to achieving world peace.

Tribute To Laura Briley

You can do it. Do it for the babies. It is all about the babies . . .
                                                                    —Laura Briley

Laura Briley, founder of Working Group on Rights for Children Living in Children's Homes, was also the founder and former president of Pikler/Lóczy USA. In addition, Laura was a champion of peace, a great humanitarian, and role model. She was our hero and inspired us by her example.

Laura had two special loves that were dear to her heart: World Forum Foundation and Pikler. She empowered anyone she came in contact with and saw their potential as human beings. As an extraordinary leader, she held all accountable and helped to redefine thier mission and purpose on this earth.

She got her way because she addressed us with compassion, and you couldn't help but feel dignified when you were with her:

She made each one of us feel important and was adored by her staff who would frequently exclaim, *"I want to grow up to be Laura!"* or *"Laura always had faith that I could be more than I believed I could be."*

Her relationship with those of us who worked with her was warm, caring, friendly, and extremely respectful. Dozens under her employment have expressed their gratitude at how Laura had not only given them jobs, but also gave them free childcare and paid for their college education so that they could earn a degree, thus allowing them to have a chance at a life with dignity.

She taught them about caring for babies with respect, and in turn, they also became respectful toward one another.

Laura once visited Romania while vacationing through Eastern Europe. When she encountered the thousands of orphans who were longing to be held, whose smiles were vanishing from their faces, she knew that her true journey had begun and that if she could make a difference in the life of just *one* child, her life would have been worthwhile.

Laura shared her story of Orphanage 5 in Romania. Babies deprived of any type of care, who were losing the glimmer in their eyes and who were fed only if they had enough strength to cry out from hunger, were considered objects that were merely in the way and unnecessary.

They were called the irrecoverable children.

Laura spoke of the countless hours she invested in creating a beautiful and nurturing space, the professionals she enrolled as volunteers in her purpose to give these children a brighter beginning: Laura was making a difference in the lives of hundreds of little ones.

She knew that her life was to be shared with the very young and that if children were to grow up and make a positive difference in the world, they needed to be raised with love, care, and respect.

During her quest for a healthy upbringing, she discovered the Pikler Institute and became immersed in Dr. Emmi Pikler's approach of considering the baby as an active participant of his/her care since his/her first day of life. She became passionate about this approach because she saw the positive impact that it had on children, and she trained her staff in Tulsa, where she lived and worked, according to Dr. Pikler's principles.

Because of her dedication to this child-rearing philosophy, she was chosen to represent Pikler in the United States and, in 1991, founded Pikler-Lóczy USA, a nonprofit corporation. In 2003, its board of directors was established. Over the years, Laura worked tirelessly with many directors of residential nurseries worldwide and managed to change some of the ways that babies were being treated. She traveled globally presenting on the Pikler approach, and many ambassadors, ministers of education, diplomats, and first ladies opened their doors and their hearts to her. Indeed, nothing could stop her, as she was determined to change the world one baby at a time, nurturing one and making an impact to many.

Laura's influence and the effects of her actions extend to thousands upon thousands. She has had a ripple effect of love, and her dream was that one day every baby on this planet would be treated with respect.

This book is dedicated to her memory. And in the words of the youngest ever Nobel Prize laureate, Malala Yousafzai, *"Let us make our future now, and let us make our dreams tomorrow's reality."*

Author Biographies

Elsa Chahin is an in-demand speaker, writer, teacher, and infant-toddler consultant, with more than twenty years' experience working with infants, children, and youth populations around the globe. Chahin has served as a keynote speaker and presenter at over 80 national and international conferences and seminars on the topic of caring for babies with respect. She has also been featured as an online parenting expert for early childhood development and special needs topics.

As one of only two certified and accredited Pikler® Trainers in North America, she is currently president of the internationally renowned nonprofit corporation, Pikler/Loczy USA, through which she carries on the mission of Dr. Emmi Pikler, that of raising healthy, happy children. With extensive training in the field, Chahin, raised in both Mexico and the United States, is also bilingual, as well as conversational in French.

A skilled translator who has worked with multicultural students, including at-risk, orphaned, abandoned, and learning-disabled children, she is a gifted facilitator that brings her expertise in her consulting and advisory positions to new parents and professionals.

In addition to being a staunch advocate of early childhood education and development, Chahin, a former professional ballerina who brings her knowledge of movement to her work, is a working group leader for World Forum Foundation, RIE (Resources for Infant Educarers) associate, and a PITC trainer. Her family is her driving force.

Anna Tardos, president of the Pikler-Lóczy Association Hungary, is a child psychologist by education, who also worked as an assistant teacher in a university, as well as a high school teacher after the Hungarian Revolution of 1956. It was during this time that she started to carry out studies based on regular observations at the Lóczy Infants' Home.

After the birth of her third child, Tardos stopped teaching and, in 1961, worked exclusively at Lóczy with her mother, Dr. Emmi Pikler. Besides her work at the institute, which included research, pedagogical work, and management, Tardos regularly held lectures and seminars about the development, care, and education of infants and young children, not only in Budapest, but also in Austria, Belgium, Finland, France, Germany, Italy, Spain, Sweden, Northern Ireland, USA, and Switzerland.

In 1998, Tardos became the director of the Pikler Institute, succeeding Dr. Emmi Pikler, Dr. Judit Falk, and Dr. Gabriella Püspöky, respectively. Continuing to carry on the work of her mother, Tardos has set up English-language Pikler trainings and English-language lectures. She has published over sixty articles in five languages, and Tardos is also author, coauthor, or editor of many handbooks and curricula. She is an honorary member of the French division of the international professional organization, World Association for Infant Mental Health and of the University of Liege.

Today she provides support to the Pikler Daycare Center and Pikler parent-child groups. As the president of one of the two closely cooperating nonprofit organizations, the Hungarian Pikler-Lóczy Association and the Lóczy Foundation for Children, Tardos actively participates in organizing and teaching courses offered at Lóczy and abroad.

Photos of Anna and Elsa

Contributors

Joy Amulya, EdD (Nepal study), has directed a number of multiyear evaluation projects and developed learning systems for international and domestic initiatives focused on human development and sustainable change. She has a doctorate in human development from Harvard University.

Jason Scott Bell is a recipient of the American Academy of Poets Prize. Among the publications he has contributed to are *Harpers*, *The Paris Review*, and *The St. Petersburg Times*.

Sjoukje Borbély, PhD, was born in the Netherlands. After working at the Pikler Institute for twelve years, she worked at the psychological department of the Training College for Teachers of the Handicapped. She is currently working as a child psychologist, especially interested in children with special needs and their parents.

Denise Da Ros-Voseles, PhD, is a professor and chair of the early childhood program at Northeastern State University, where she teaches graduate and undergraduate infant and toddler development courses. She is the Pikler/Lóczy USA secretary of board of directors and is also the coauthor of *Being with Babies: Understanding and Responding to the Infants in Your Care.*

Pia Dögl was born in Bonn, Germany, in 1972. As an educator, she has worked for educational institutions and as a freelance consultant. She was a founding member and is on the management committee of the Kinder Haus for neglected and abused children in Berlin, www. beginningwell.org.

Amy Gedal Douglass, PhD (Nepal study), leads monitoring, evaluation, and research projects in the United States and Asia to facilitate data use for decision-making and continuous learning and improvement. She has a doctorate in public health from George Washington University.

Freema Davis, MA (Nepal study), founded Global Family Village in the United States in 2007. She has been working with Global Family Village-Nepal, a local NGO specifically to create and pilot a sustainable, community-supported model of care for orphaned and abandoned children.

Judit Falk, MD (1922–2010), worked at the Pikler Institute for forty-eight years, 12 of those as its director. She published twenty-one scientific studies in Hungarian and dozens more in seven different languages. Dr. Falk was an expert who spoke at conferences around the world, gave training for caregivers, and was active in establishing and managing several other professional organizations.

Joyce Gallardo has been an early childhood educator for nearly three decades and is the director of Los Amiguitos, a home-based nursery-kindergarten in Harlemville, New York. She has completed advanced training at the Pikler Institute, Budapest, and has worked for many years with the Waldorf School movement in Ecuador.

Diane Harkins, PhD, is an early childhood specialist with the San Francisco-based Center for Child and Family Studies at WestEd. Her current projects include training and technical assistance to infant-toddler programs in California's rural counties. In addition, Harkins studied at the Pikler Institute in 2007 and 2008.

Stella Henson is the author of *Memories of Thompson Orphanage* and has worked in both the private sector and in government, including for Virginia's Social Services; Raleigh, North Carolina's School for the Blind; and the U.S. Postal Service.

Katalin Hevesi began working at Lóczy in 1963 and has been spreading the Piklerian approach to Hungarian and French infants' homes. In addition, she has held seminars for the French Pikler-Lóczy Association in France and in Belgium for ten years and currently works in the archives of the Hungarian Pikler-Lóczy Association.

Éva Kálló (1943–2015) began teaching developmental and educational psychology at the Caregivers' Training in Hungary in 1973 and worked at Lóczy as a group pedagogue for nearly forty years. Her research has appeared in publications, at scientific meetings of the Psychological Association of the Hungarian Academy of Sciences, and at various conferences in Hungary and abroad. She coauthored the book *The Development of Free Play* with Györgyi Balog, which has been published in Hungarian, German, English, and most recently, Spanish.

Natasha Khazanov, PhD, is a neuropsychologist, psychotherapist, and creator of the SMARTT parenting program. She also is an associate clinical professor at UCSF School of Medicine. Her interest in the neurobiology of trauma led her to forensics, where she served as an expert witness in over **80** criminal cases.

Peter Mangione, PhD, is codirector of WestEd Center for Child and Family Studies. He provides leadership in the development of comprehensive training resources for infant and toddler caregivers and the evaluation of early childhood programs and services. Mangione received a doctorate in education and human development from the University of Rochester and completed a postdoctoral fellowship at the Max-Planck-Institute of Psychiatry in Munich, Germany. He serves on the advisory board of Pikler/Lóczy Fund USA.

Ruth Mason is an Israel-based journalist who has written extensively about parents and children, including articles on RIE and the Pikler approach. She wrote the weekly column, "Parenting," in the *Jerusalem Post* for seven years and is studying to be a Pikler pedagogue.

Etienne Moine was born in France has been living in Ecuador since 1978. With industrial engineering and business administration degrees, Etienne is administrative director of Casa de los Niños. An avid photographer and filmmaker, he codirected the documentary *GRANDIR: Loving and Respecting children, An Everyday Challenge*. He's a speaker at national and international conferences. His photos can be enjoyed in part three, **chapter 3.4**, http://fundacionami.org. ec/wp/.

Oleg I. Palmov, PhD, is an associate professor, Department of Mental Health and Early Childhood Intervention, Faculty of Psychology, St. Petersburg State University, with a focus on young children and families, children with severe mental and physical disabilities, and institutionalized children and their early social-emotional experience and caregiving environment. He has promoted the Pikler approach for over ten years through academic courses in university and postgraduate training programs for orphanage caregivers and is an author in the areas of improved interventions in orphanages, applied developmental psychology, and early intervention.

Barbara Rios-Brenes is director of Children's Hope Lodge of the American Cancer Society in Puerto Rico. She is a member of the World Forum Foundation Working Group on the Rights for Children Living in Children's Homes.

Elke-Maria Rischke has worked as a Waldorf kindergarten teacher for more than three decades, having founded four kindergartens in various towns in Germany. She was a founding member of the Kinder Haus for neglected and abused children in Berlin. She also holds seminars and training courses in Germany and other European countries.

Intisar Shareef, EdD, is department chair of early childhood education at Contra Costa College in San Pablo, California. She coauthored the publication *Practice on Building Bridges*, a companion resource to *Diversity in Early Care and Education*, fifth edition. Shareef received a doctorate degree in early childhood education from Nova University and has taught at all levels from preschool through college. She serves on the executive board of directors of Pikler/Lóczy USA.

Prof. Kishor Shrestha, PhD (Nepal study), has over three decades of experience in conducting research in the field of early childhood and elementary education in Nepal and Asia region. He was a steering committee member of the Asia-Pacific Regional Network for Early Childhood (ARNEC) from 2008 to 2011. Kishor has a doctorate in early childhood education from the University of Delhi, India.

Ronald Ssentuuwa is global child advocate working with SOS Children's Village Uganda as a project manager on Alternative Care Consortium on Systems Strengthening (ACCoSS). He has also worked as programs manager, Children International, in Uganda, and is a member of the Global Leaders for Young Children World Forum.

Agnes Szanto, PhD, had early contact with Dr. Emmi Pikler, who was her family's pediatrician when she was born. She has lived in France since 1956 and received a master's degree and doctorate in psychology in the research of the psychomotor development of young children. A professor of early childhood development at universities in France, Belgium, Italy, and Argentina, Szanto is also a keynote speaker at international conferences. She is a founding member and vice president of the Pikler-Lóczy Association of France and of the International Pikler Association. She has authored several books that have been translated into several languages.

Borbála Szentpétery is an occupational therapist who worked at the Pikler residential nursery and is currently working at the Pikler Daycare Center facilitating parent-child groups. Together with Dr. Sjoukje Borbély, they produced the film *Children with Special*

Needs Living in the Lóczy—Additional Care and the lecture Special Education within Lóczy—An Interesting Challenge.

Gabriela Tejeda has been national director of VIFAC in Mexico since 2002 and has over twenty years experience working for various nonprofit organizations that care for women, adolescents, and children living in residential care. In 2007, she studied at the Pikler Institute under Anna Tardos, gaining and a new and comprehensive insight into what children being reared in children's homes truly need.

Maria del Carmen Vásquez is president of Amigos de La Vida Foundation, a founding member of Ecuador's Network of Children's Homes and Network for the Well Treatment of Children in the Tumbaco Valley. As director of La Casa de los Niños, she provides opportunities for respectful care and nurturing for children zero to four years of age that come from a difficult beginning, including abandonment, abuse, chronic illness, and disabilities. She is often invited as speaker at national and international symposiums.

Mária Vincze, MD (1925–2009), joined the team at the Pikler Institute in 1962, first as a pediatrician and later in the role of assistant director. During her nearly thirty years there, she worked on daily life, the family connections of the children living at Lóczy, and research work. Vincze wrote several texts on the Pikler approach and worked with Genevieve Appell and Judit Falk on the film *Babies and Children with Each Other*. To find out about Casa Ami, http://fundacionami.org.ec/wp/.

Kathryn Whetten is a professor of public policy and global health with additional appointments in community and family medicine and nursing. She is the director of the Center for Health Policy and Inequalities, with a focus on the understanding of health disparities in the United States and around the globe. In addition, she uses her research results to develop and test interventions that might improve outcomes.

Caroline Wilcox, MA, is an educator, who, for the last sixteen years, has taught upper elementary school. During summer, she teaches and trains teachers in Egypt and Fiji as the director of Curriculum Development for Global Classrooms for Peace.

Glossary Of People And Places

Geneviève Appell, *psychologist*, is a recognized early childhood authority, and participated in research commissioned by the World Health Organization. She has authored books and made educational films with the Pikler Institute in Budapest, including her co-authorship with Dr. Myriam David of the book: *LÓCZY, An unusual approach to mothering.* Appell was awarded the Emmi Pikler Award in 2014 for her invaluable contribution. She lives in France.

Myriam David, MD, *psychoanalyst, pediatrician, and French psychiatrist* (1917–2004), received a scholarship from the World Health Organization in 1962 to conduct a study on "Children Separated from Their Mothers for the First Three Months of Life and Up Their Four Years." David wrote numerous articles and several books, including *Lóczy: An Unusual Approach to Mothering*, which David coauthored with Appell. David also founded two institutions for children: Soisy Family Centre sur Seine (therapeutic foster care) in 1966 and the Rothschild Foundation in 1976, renamed, in 2006, the Myriam David Centre.

Magda Gerber, *infant-toddler specialist* (1910–2007), and her two youngest children were under the care of Dr. Pikler before WWII. After the Second World War, Gerber and Dr. Pikler remained friends. In 1978, Gerber and Tom Forrest, MD, cofounded Resources for Infant Educarers (RIE), which is based on Dr. Pikler's principles.

Elsa Gindler, *pioneer in somatic bodywork* (1885–1961), originated a school of movement education. Her emphasis was on self-awareness by exploring oneself during walking, sitting, and standing, as well as other movements, carried out daily.

Bernard Golse, MD, *pediatrician, child psychiatrist, and psychoanalyst* (member of the *Association Psychanalytique* *de France* [French Psychoanalytic Association]) is the head of pediatric psychiatry services at the *Hôpital Necker – Enfants Malades* [Children's hospital] in Paris. As professor of child and adolescent psychiatry, he teaches at the University René Descartes in Paris. Golse is the Founder of the French division of WAIMH (World Association for Infant Mental Health); former member of the *Conseil Supérieur de l'Adoption (CSA)* [French Superior Council of Adoption]; former president of *the Conseil National pour l'Accès aux Origines Personnelles (CNAOP)* [National Council for the Access to Personal Origins]; member of the *Conseil Scientifique de la Société Française de Psychiatrie de l'Enfant et de l'Adolescent et des Disciplines alliées (SFPEADA)* [French Scientific Council of Child and Adolescent Psychiatry and Associated Disciplines]. Currently, he is also president of the French Pikler-Lóczy Association, and President of the *Association Européenne de Psychopathologie de l'Enfant et de l'Adolescent (AEPEA)* [European Association of Child and Adolescent Psychopathology], and author of *L'esser-bebè.*

Janet Gonzalez-Mena, MA, is an author, consultant in early childhood education, and former community college instructor. More recently, she has been studying the Pikler approach to infant-toddler care and has visited the Pikler Institute several times. Infants have been an important part of Janet's life, having raised five children of her own and having studied the field of infant-toddler caregiving for the last forty years. Gonzalez-Mena serves on the board of trustees of Pikler/Lóczy USA.

Elfriede Hengstenberg, *pioneer in somatic bodywork* (1892–1992), worked as a gymnastic teacher at a Montessori school in Berlin and also trained with Elsa Gindler and Heinrich Jacoby. Pikler invited Hengstenberg to come to Budapest in 1934, 1935, 1936, and both shared the vision of children being able to discover and develop their motor skills independently.

Judit (Jutka) Kelemen, *lead group caregiver at Lóczy* trained as a health-care professional and has been working at the Pikler Institute and Pikler Daycare Center for thirty years. Kelemen is a prolific speaker and sought-after presenter at national and international conferences. Topics of her lectures have included *changing the diaper of a mobile infant, relationships and conflicts among children; the development of play; the role of the adult in the child's play; the caregiver's professional development at the Pikler Institute;* among many others.

Zsuzsa Libertiny, *executive pedagogue of the Pikler Daycare Center*, became closely acquainted with the Piklerian ideas with the birth of her first child (1997). An employee of the Pikler Institute in 2002, Libertiny was responsible for family programs and parent-child groups. She left Lóczy for a few years to work in Canada supporting newly immigrated parents with young children. After her return to the Lóczy team, she resumed her previous role, as well as joining the day-care center as a pedagogue. Since 2009, Libertiny regularly participates as a lecturer both in Hungary and abroad. Her topics encompass the everyday work with children, the support for families, day-care centers, and residential institutions.

Eszter Mózes, *author, researcher, clinical child psychologist, and director of the Lóczy Foundation for Children*, has been working together with the Pikler/Lóczy team since 1988. Her two areas of special interest and research are early manifestations of sense of humor in the youngest age and the detailed way in which the adult's role changes in parallel with the development of the child. She has been working with the Early Intervention Centre in Budapest since 1999. She currently facilitates trainings for the Lóczy Foundation for Children in French, Spanish, and Hungarian.

Klara Pap, *illustrator*, was the recipient of the Emmi Pikler Award in 2016 for her valuable contributions to the Pikler approach. Pap worked closely with Dr. Pikler by sketching the natural progression of children's gross motor development as well as the tender moments of care at Lóczy, the infants' home in Budapest, Hungary.

Marian Reismann, *photographer* (1911–1991). It was in her shop that Reismann first met Dr. Emmi Pikler. Pikler visited Reismann's shop seeking a photographer to take photos of her young patients whom she saw as a family pediatrician in Budapest. They continued to work together at the residential nursery. Reismann was part of the 2001 exhibition at the National Museum in Washington (USA), "Picturing Progress: Hungarian Women Photographers 1900–1945." Her photos are included in a number of books, including *Give me Time* (Pikler) and *Emmi Pikler, More Than a Pediatrician* (Czimmek).

Ute Strub, *physiotherapist and movement pedagogue*, was a student of Elfriede Hengstenberg. Strub worked closely with Dr. Pikler since the '70s and helped translate Pikler's books from Hungarian into German. She currently works alongside Anna Tardos offering Pikler trainings internationally. Strub was presented with the Emmi Pikler Award in 2015. Her book with Elsa Chahin, *Ways of Being with Oneself and with Children*, will be published in 2018.

Lóczy Foundation for Children is presided by Jutka Kelemen and directed by Eszter Mózes. Its responsibilities include financial support to the Pikler Daycare Center to purchase furniture and play equipment, maintaining the building where it is housed, promoting the Pikler knowledge, as well as offering courses in different languages (Hungarian, Portuguese, Spanish, English, and French).

Pikler Daycare Center, opened in 2006, housed in the same home as Lóczy (the Pikler residential nursery), offers a weekday service for children ages five months to three years old. Its mission is conserving the practical applications of the Pikler pedagogy. Many of the caregivers worked in the residential nursery and are well versed in the Pikler pedagogy.

Pikler-Lóczy Association Hungary (MPLT). Anna Tardos is the president and Zsuzsa Libertiny, the vice president. Its mission is to promote Pikler's heritage. Responsibilities include preserving the archive that includes films, photographs, and documents written during the sixty-five of years of the Pikler Institute, as well as publishing books and educational material. This is a place where professionals can conduct research. This association is in charge of all the Pikler courses offered in the German language and supports the Pikler Daycare Center as well, www.pikler.hu.

Pikler Institute was established in 1946 as the *Infants' Home of Budapest.* The infants' home was operating from 1946 to 2011. In the first few decades, it accommodated children zero to three years of age, later zero to six. It also operated as a National Methodological Institute.

Pikler/Lóczy USA (PLUSA) is a 501(c)3 nonprofit corporation founded by Laura Briley in 1991. PLUSA promotes respectful and harmonious relationships between the youngest child and the adult. Its mission is to support the adult through service, training, and research in USA and internationally. The focus is to preserve the competence, autonomy, and integrity of the young child, as formulated, studied, and practiced by Hungarian pediatrician Emmi Pikler, MD (1902–1984), in order to ensure the child's well-being in families and in group settings. Its vision is a world where all children are cared for with respect, www.pikler.org.

The Pikler Collection is a website that aims to share as much information as possible on the work of Dr. Emmi Pikler in the English language. It includes a collection of links, videos, and articles for anyone searching information on Pikler and the Pikler approach, http://thepiklercollection.weebly.com.

Bibliography

Borbély, Sjoukje. Sp*ecial Education within Loczy: An Interesting Challenge*. Published by The Hungarian Pikler-Lóczy Association and Emmi Pikler, Stichting, Netherlands. ISBN 978-90-807225-3-8.

David, Myriam and Appell, Genevieve. LOCZY An Unusual Approach to Mothering. Published by Pikler-Lóczy Association for Young Children Budapest ([1973, 1996] 2001). ISBN 978-9630053914.

Falk, Judit. "Why Should We Lay the Infant in the Prone Position?" (also known as "Why We Don't Put Babies in the Prone Position") *Child and Youth Medical Journal.* Published by Le Promenade, Budapest, and Pikler-Lóczy Association for Young Children, Budapest (2011).

Falk, Judit and Vincze Maria. *Bathing the Baby: The Art of Care*. Published by Pikler-Lóczy Association for Young Children Budapest (2006).

Falk, Judit and Pikler Emmi. Data on the Social Adjustment of Children Reared in our Institute. Emmi Pikler International Public Foundation.

Falk, Judit and Pikler, Emmi. Data on the Social Adjustment of Children Reared in our Institute. Emmi Pikler International Public Foundation.

Grey, Peter. *Free to LEARN: Why Unleashing the Instinct to Play Will Make Our Children Happier, More Self-Reliant, and Better Students for Life*. Basic Books, New York, New York (2015). ISBN-13: 978-0465084999, ISBN-10: 0465084990.

Groos, Karl. *The Play of Man* (trans. Elizabeth L. Baldwin). New York: Appleton (1901).

Henson Griggs Batson, Stella. *Memories of Thompson Orphanage*, Xlibris, 2014. ISBN-10: 1499065582, ISBN-13: 978-1499065589.

Kálló, Éva and Balog, Gyorgyi. *The Origins of Free Play*. Published by Pikler-Lóczy Association for Young Children Budapest (2005). ISBN-13 9789638667120.

Kálló, Éva. *Name and Sign*. Emmi Pikler International Public Foundation.

Montessori, Maria. *The Absorbent Mind*. New York, Holt, Rinehart and Winston (1967). ASIN: B00ZBBLZF2

Anna Tardos (ed.). *Bringing Up and Providing Care for Infants and Toddlers in an Institution*. Published by Pikler-Lóczy Association for Young Children Budapest (2007).

Mary Alice Roche (ed.). "Story of Emmi Pikler 1902–1984" (bulletin). Published by Sensory Awareness Foundation, USA (1994).

Pikler, Emmi. *Unfolding of Infants' Natural Gross Motor Development* (illustrated by Klara Pap). Published by Resources for Infant Educarers (2006). ISBN 9781892560070.

Pikler, Emmi *Laßt mir Zeit. Give me time.* (with Anna Tardos). Pflaum, München 2001 / 3. ISBN 3-7905-0842-X.

Pikler, Emmi, *Friedliche Babys - zufriedene Mütter, Peaceful Baby - Contented Mothers*. Freiburg 2008/9. ISBN 978-3-451-04986-6.

Szanto-Feder, Agnes (ed.). *Lóczy ¿Un Nuevo Paradigma? El Instituto Pikler Es Un Espejo De Multiples Facetas*. EDIUNC 2006, ISBN 950-39-0200-2.

Spitz, R. A. (1945). Hospitalism—An Inquiry into the Genesis of Psychiatric Conditions in Early Childhood. Psychoanalytic Study of the Child, 1, 53-74.

Szanto-Feder, Agnes. *"Una Mirada adulta sobre el niño en acción; El sentido del movimiento en la protoinfancia"*, EDICIONES CINCO, Buenos Aires, 2014, ch. 1, pp. 54–59.

Tardos, Anna. "Let the Infant Play by Himself as Well." *The First Years. New Zealand Journal of Infant and Toddler Education*, vol. 14, Issue 1, 2012 pp. 4–9.

Tardos, Anna. "Introducing the Piklerian Development Approach: History and Principles, Researching the Infant." *The Signal, Newsletter of the World Association for Infant Mental Health*, vol. 18. No . 3-4 / July–December 2010 (pp. 3–4, pp. 9–14).

Myriam David. *"Le Bébé, Ses parents, Leurs Soignats,"* Editions Erès, no. 5 – 1997, France.

Winnicott, D. W. (1957). *The Child and the Family.* Tavistock Publications. ASIN: B00007IT61Y

Winnicott, D.W. (1953). *Transitional Objects and Transitional Phenomena—A Study of the First Not-Me Possession.* Int. J. Psycho-Anal., 34:89-97.

Books inspired by Dr. Emmi Pikler
and the Pikler® Pedagogy

Emmi Pikler, More than a Pediatrician, Czimmek, 2015, Munich, ISBN 978-3-931428-20-4.

Respect: A Practitioner's Guide to Calm & Nurturing Infant Care & Education (Christie), Childspace Early Childhood Institute, New Zealand, ISBN10 0473185547, ISBN13 9780473185541.

"Pädagogik der frühen Kindheit. Die Bedeutung von Emmi Pikler und Heinrich Jacoby" (Riethmüller), GRIN Verlag 2010, ASIN: B007GY04WC.

Being with Infants and Toddlers: A Curriculum That Works for Caregivers (Kovach, Patrick). ISBN-10: 0615635164, ISBN-13: 978-0615635163.

Being with Babies: Understanding and Responding to the Infants in Your Care (Kovach, Da Ros-Voseles). Gryphon House2008, ISBN-10: 0876590628, ISBN-13: 978-0876590621.

Your Self-Confident Baby: How to Encourage Your Child's Natural Abilities—From the Very Start, 2012 (Gerber, Johnson), 2003, ISBN-10: 1118158792, ISBN-13: 978-1118158791.

Dear Parent: Caring for Infants with Respect (Gerber), Resources for Infant Educarers, 2003, ISBN-10: 1892560062, ISBN-13: 978-1892560063.

Baby Knows Best: Raising a Confident and Resourceful Child, The RIE Way (Salomon), Little, Brown and Company, 2015, ISBN-10: 0316219193, ISBN-13: 978-0316219198.

Made in the USA
Columbia, SC
10 April 2022

58769565R00176